Conscientization and Deschooling

Conscientization and Deschooling

FREIRE'S AND ILLICH'S PROPOSALS
FOR RESHAPING SOCIETY

by
JOHN L. ELIAS

THE WESTMINSTER PRESS
Philadelphia

Grateful acknowledgment is made to Harper &
Row, Publishers, Inc., for quotations from *Tools
for Conviviality*, by Ivan Illich, Vol. 47 of *World
Perspectives*, planned and edited by Ruth Nanda
Anshen, copyright © 1973 by Ivan Illich.

Book Design by Dorothy Alden Smith

Published by The Westminster Press ®
Philadelphia, Pennsylvania

PRINTED IN THE UNITED STATES OF AMERICA

Library of Congress Cataloging in Publication Data

Elias, John L   1933–
    Conscientization and deschooling.

    Bibliography: p.
    1. Sociology, Christian (Catholic)—History.
2. Social change. 3. Education—Philosophy.
4. Illich, Ivan D. 5. Freire, Paulo, 1921–
I. Title.
BT738.E39   301.24   76–20618
ISBN 0–664–20787–1

Contents

Foreword

Two of the most influential thinkers in recent years in the area of social and educational thought have been Paulo Freire and Ivan Illich. Though these men write out of the perspective of the Third World, their influence has extended beyond that world into more industrialized nations. The impact of their ideas has been felt far beyond the area of educational thought. Religious thinkers, political activists, community workers, social scientists, environmentalists, and others have shown a keen interest in the proposals of these men for reshaping society.

Two concepts lie at the heart of the thinking of these two men. For Freire, the concept is *conscientization.* This is the process by which a group of people become aware of the cultural context in which they live and become challenged to work actively to bring about change for the better. For Illich, the concept is *deschooling.* The elimination of schools from society is for Illich the necessary condition for freeing people from their addiction to manipulative and oppressive institutions.

My analysis of Freire and Illich has led me to an inescapable conclusion: these men can be best understood from the perspective of the religious tradition in which they are situated. Both men are Catholic humanistic thinkers. This tradition has provided them with principles about the nature of man, society, politics, and education, to which they can appeal in making proposals for reshaping society. Though there

9

are differences in the approaches that these men take to certain problems and issues, the many similarities in their views can be traced, at least in part, to the common religious views that they hold.

This book is a work of comparison, contrast, analysis, evaluation, and criticism. Steeped in the same tradition as Freire and Illich, I feel that I have an advantage in presenting this interpretative and critical study. Most articles on Freire and Illich have not commented on the religious dimension of their thought. It is my contention that no adequate evaluation and analysis of their contribution is possible unless serious attention is given to the Catholic dimension of their thought.

A number of people have given me assistance in the writing of this book. Personal conversations I have had with Paulo Freire and Ivan Illich have been invaluable. I am grateful to James E. McClellan, Professor of Education at the State University of New York at Albany, for initially suggesting the theme of the book. Peter Bachrach, Professor of Political Science; William Cutler, Assistant Professor of History and Education; B. Paul Komisar, Professor of Educational Foundations; and Leonard Wacks, Associate Professor of Educational Foundations, all of Temple University, have offered helpful criticisms. D. Campbell Wyckoff, Professor of Religious Education, Princeton Theological Seminary, read the manuscript and made perceptive suggestions for its final revision.

My deepest gratitude is to my wife, Eleanor Flanigan. She alone has shared with me the entire adventure of writing this book. I dedicate this book to her and to our daughter Rebecca, who came to us during the time of its writing.

1
Religious Reformers

Two radical and different approaches to educational and social reform have been proposed in recent years. One is the
theory of education through conscientization expounded by
Paulo Freire, the Brazilian educator, now in exile from his
native country. The other is the theoretical and practical
program for deschooling society presented by Ivan Illich, the
cofounder of the Centro Intercultural de Documentacion
(CIDOC) in Cuernavaca, Mexico. Today these two thinkers
are at the center of educational controversy in many countries of the world. Their ideas are well known in both Latin
and North America. Recent educational reform proposals in
Peru (*Ley general*, 1972) have been greatly influenced by
their thought. The writings of Illich have long been discussed
in the United States and Canada, where he has often appeared for lectures, conferences, and symposia. Paulo Freire,
though less well known in North America, is becoming more
and more influential in circles proposing educational and
social reform. Interest in Freire is especially strong among
adult educators (Grabowski, 1972; Lloyd, 1972) and religious
educators (Clasby, 1971; Warford, 1974).

In this work I intend to make comparisons and contrasts
between these two influential thinkers and to present a critical analysis of their thought. Before embarking upon that
venture, however, I will attempt to situate them both in their
proper historical and intellectual context. I will do this by
first briefly tracing the background of each man. Secondly,

11

the major intellectual influences on their thinking will be presented. Finally, there will be a description of the influences that each man has had on the other. Though Illich and Freire do not look upon themselves as co-workers, they admit to a close personal and intellectual friendship.

Paulo Freire

Paulo Freire was born in 1921 in Recife, a center of great poverty in northeast Brazil. In the early years of his life, he experienced firsthand the struggle against poverty and hunger when the depression of 1929 struck his middle-class family. As a result of this situation, Freire fell two years behind in his schoolwork. Some of his teachers diagnosed his condition as mental retardation. Freire was deeply affected by this experience of poverty and vowed because of it to work among the poor of the northeast to try to improve their lot.

Freire studied law and philosophy at the University of Pernambuco. Following his legal studies, he worked as a labor-union lawyer among the people of the slums. It was through this work that Freire became involved in literacy training. By 1947 Freire had developed his great interest in adult literacy education among the poor in the northeast. His involvement with literacy education between 1947 and 1959 caused him to become dissatisfied with traditional methods for dealing with illiteracy. These methods assume an authoritative relationship between teacher and pupil, and Freire observed a prejudiced point of view within the traditional primer. (Wagley, 1971, p. 192.) Even after he was appointed professor of the history and philosophy of education at the University of Recife in 1959, Freire maintained his interest in adult literacy education. In this capacity he was successful in involving students in his work with adult literacy projects.

In the early 1960's Freire became increasingly involved with various reform movements in northeast Brazil. De Kadt (1970), a historian of these reform movements, notes that they did not attract a large following; they were also short-lived, coming to an abrupt end with the coup of 1964. These attempts at reform centered around the Popular Culture Movement, of which Freire was a member. Students dominated the Popular Culture Movement which was an attempt to democratize the culture through discussions on such themes as nationalism, remission of profits, development, and literacy. The movement also attempted to raise class-consciousness and to increase the popular vote.

The early 1960's also saw the beginnings of rural and urban unions in the northeast. About 1,300 farm workers' unions were founded within twelve months. Farm workers' strikes in Pernambuco in 1963 are an index to the success of this effort. The first strike involved 84,000 workers, the second, 230,000 workers. The Popular Culture Movement, together with the Supervisory Agency for Agrarian Reform (SUPRA), was able to effect this mobilization.

Literacy, however, was central to all the reform movements in northeast Brazil. Only literates were permitted to vote. Voting according to the interests of the patrons or owners of plantations had long been considered a political duty for peasants. With the formation of Peasants Leagues under Francisco Julião (1972) in the 1950's, the people became more aware of their power to vote. Weffort (1969, p. 12), in his introduction to Freire's *Educação como prática da liberdade,* pointed out the importance of the literacy movement in Brazil at this time. Weffort shows that there was a high correlation between illiteracy and socioeconomic stagnation. He charged the elites of the country with purposely fostering this situation.

The history of Freire's literacy efforts in Brazil is a brief one. The Popular Culture Movement made use of visual aids to dramatize various issues under discussion. The results were so satisfactory that Freire decided to use the same types of methods with his literacy training.

Weffort (1969) gives the year 1963 as the real beginning of the Freire literacy movement as such. In the beginning, the Alliance for Progress was interested in Freire's experiment, which took place in Angicos, a city of the Rio Grande do Norte. Dulles (1970, p. 216) states that Freire received some help from the United States Aid for International Development program (AID). The results of this experiment were impressive. Three hundred workers learned to read and write in forty-five days!

In the earlier stages of his experiment, Freire was working directly with the Popular Culture Movement, whose leadership was Roman Catholic. Gradually members of the Communist Party became influential among the rank and file. It was partly in reaction to this development that Freire transferred his populist method to the cultural extension service of the University of Recife (de Kadt, 1970, pp. 102–104). Movimento de Base (MED), another program for literacy training, supported by church and government, became radicalized at the same time. This was another reason for Freire's decision to transfer his method to the university.

Freire's literacy program was extended to the entire nation after June, 1963, when Paulo de Tarso, a friend of Freire, became Minister of Education. He was a member of Catholic Action groups, a liberal reformer, and popular among student leaders. De Tarso was instrumental in getting Freire's method used in the entire country. Through him Freire was appointed director of the national literacy campaign. Between June 1963 and March 1964, training programs for adult literacy educators were developed in almost all the state capitals. In Guanabara State alone, almost 6,000 people were enrolled. There were also courses in the states of Rio Grande do Norte, São Paolo, Bahia, Sergipe, and Rio Grande do Sul. These training courses were developed within eight months, with college students serving most vigorously as coordinators.

The 1964 plan was to establish 20,000 discussion groups, which would be equipped to teach approximately 20 million illiterates. There were to be thirty persons in each group for a three-month period. This national literacy program was modeled after the example of Cuba, which had almost eliminated illiteracy through a massive literacy campaign (Bowles, 1971).

The federal literacy campaign sponsored both the efforts of Freire and the Movement for Basic Education, the church-based endeavor headed by Marina Bandiera. Freire's work was separate from that of the MEB, but there was a great similarity between them (de Kadt, 1970, pp. 102–103). The MEB still continues in Brazil under Bandiera's leadership, but its government subsidy is shrinking. It is being eclipsed by the government's own Brazilian Literacy Movement (MOBRAL). The MEB prepared a catechism in 1963 entitled *Viver e lutar* (To Live Is to Struggle). It consisted of thirty lessons, realistically illustrated with photographs, geared to the experience of the peasant and his actual situation. It started from assumptions very similar to those of Freire. From late 1962 onward, a certain amount of give-and-take occurred, especially in the northeast, among the various literacy programs.

A rather widespread opposition to these literacy methods developed in conservative circles. Freire was accused of using the literacy method to spread subversive ideas. In an interview with Skidmore (1967, pp. 406–407), Freire recounts that the rightist newspaper *Globo* led the attack. The work of the MEB also came under attack, especially the small catechism.

De Kadt (1970, p. 104) contends that incitement to revolt was never the direct objective of Freire as an educator, since Freire was attempting to aid the reformist Goulart government in its efforts to bring certain political and social reforms to northeast Brazil. Freire's direct interest was democratization. He rejected authoritarian methods in education, the social palliative of welfarism, and the stifling of political expression. His work, however, undeniably contained the seeds of social revolt because it brought the people to a comprehension of the oppressive reality of their lives. In his *Pedagogy of the Oppressed* (1970a), written a number of years after the Brazilian experience, Freire indeed shows himself to be concerned with education as a means for promoting revolutionary action. *Pedagogy of the Oppressed* (1970a) may in fact be considered a handbook for revolutionary education. In proposing this revolutionary education, Freire was considering in particular the Brazilian situation, where revolution appeared to be the only means of bringing about adequate social and political change.

Nowhere in his writings does Freire give reasons for his conversion from a reformist educator to a revolutionary one. It is my view that after the coup of 1964, after Freire, with his wife and five children, was exiled from his native country, he realized most clearly that reformist activities like those he was engaged in were inadequate to bring about radical changes in the lives of the poor. No doubt the success of the revolution in Cuba had an influence on his thinking, as it has on many leftists in Latin-American countries. The success of this revolution makes more apparent the weaknesses of reform efforts in other Latin-American countries. It is probably the case that Freire's evolution from reformist to revolutionary was a gradual process reaching its culmination with the coup of 1964 and his tragic exile.

Freire's literacy campaign was brought to an abrupt end early in 1964. A bitter political struggle developed at this time between President Goulart and the military. Goulart had taken over the government in 1961 upon the resignation of President Quadros. Goulart had long been involved in leftist political reform movements. At the time of Quadros' resignation, Goulart was on a visit to Communist China, having already visited Castro's Cuba. The few years of Goulart's presidency saw the most extensive development of radical and revolutionary groups in Brazil. Many of these groups were made up of Marxists. But groups of Catholic radicals were also active in efforts at political reform, especially in the northeast.

On April 1, 1963, the conflict between Goulart and the military came to an end. The military took over the government. Miguel Arraes (1969), the governor of Pernambuco and a friend of Freire, has given a description of the coup and its aftereffects. Arraes was one of the persons forced into exile by the new government. Among many reasons given for the coup was Goulart's sympathy with experimenters on the left, such as Freire. Along with many other leaders of leftist groups, Freire was jailed. At the time of the coup, Freire was involved in the literacy campaign in Aracaju, capital of the northeast state of Sergipe. A participant in the experiment described what happened there after the coup:

> About that time, Paulo Freire's shipment of slide projectors arrived for the experiment. The soldiers broke open the boxes, believing they had intercepted machine guns for the revolution. Freire was arrested. (Diuguid, 1970, Section D-3.)

Freire spent seventy days in jail after his arrest. With some 150 other political prisoners, he was stripped of his citizen rights and sentenced into exile. With his wife and family he went to Santiago, Chile, where he worked as a UNESCO consultant and with the Agrarian Reform Training and Research Institute (ICIRA). While he was in prison, he had begun to write the account of his literacy method. He finished this book *Educação como prática da liberdade* (1967) in Chile, where it was later published in Spanish and extensively used. In Chile, Freire directed a national literacy program for the government of Eduardo Frei. In the two years of work there, his campaign won for Chile a UNESCO award for successfully eliminating illiteracy among the Chilean adult population. Efforts were made at that time to establish a permanent bureau of adult education with Freire as the director. These efforts did not materialize, and Freire left Chile to come to the United States.

Freire came to North America in 1969 at the joint invitation of Harvard University's Center for the Study of Education and Development (CSED) and the Center for the Study of Development and Social Change, located in Cambridge, Massachusetts. In 1970 Freire moved to Geneva, Switzerland, to work as a special consultant to the office of education with the World Council of Churches. He also presently works with a number of groups throughout the world that are attempting to adapt his methods to various situations. He lectured in the United States in 1972 and 1973. (At a training session at Fordham University, I met Freire and discussed with him some points about his method and about this work.) In 1973 Freire established an institute at Geneva for the purpose of coordinating efforts to develop and utilize his method in various parts of the world.

Ivan Illich

Ivan Illich was born in Vienna in 1926. His father was of a rich Dalmatian family and was a wealthy landowner and engineer. Illich received his formal education in Vienna, Salzburg, and Rome. He possesses higher degrees in philosophy and theology. After his ordination as a Roman Catholic priest and his advanced studies, he was urged to enter the Vatican diplomatic corps. He chose instead to take up work in a New York City parish.

When Illich arrived at Incarnation Parish in 1951, he found that great numbers of Puerto Ricans were moving into the predominantly Irish parish. He quickly became the advocate for these people, both in the parish and throughout New York. He quickly learned their language and began to become involved in their cultural activities. The attitudes of American Catholics toward these new immigrants disturbed him greatly. He began to write critical articles about the church and American society in general. In an early article, Illich (1956) accused the American church of smugness, bureaucracy, and chauvinism. He was especially critical of imposing Yankee values on the new immigrants. It is easy to see in this early article a foreshadowing of the type of criticisms of American society that Illich made later.

In 1957 Illich was sent to Puerto Rico by Cardinal Spellman, the Archbishop of New York. As vice-rector of the Catholic University of Puerto Rico, he was involved in training the clergy of New York and other Eastern cities for work among Puerto Ricans. At the university he formed the Institute of Intercultural Communications, through which this work was carried out. The purpose of the institute was not merely the teaching of Spanish but also an immersion into the life of the Puerto Rican people. This institute is an obvious forerunner of the Center of Intercultural Documentation (CIDOC), which Illich later established in Cuernavaca, Mexico. (In 1976, CIDOC began closing its operations except for the language school.)

Illich's work in Puerto Rico came to an end in 1961. He had been a strong proponent of the reforms introduced by Governor Munoz Marin. This incurred the enmity of conservative Catholics, including Bishop McManus of San Juan. Illich vigorously opposed the formation of the Catholic political party and supported the government's program for birth control. As a result, the bishop ordered Illich to leave Puerto Rico. He returned to New York and made plans to establish an institute elsewhere in Latin America.

It is interesting to note that Illich has consistently maintained that the church should be politically neutral and that clergymen should not get involved in running for political office. This view may perhaps make a bit more understandable the ban at CIDOC on the use of its facilities for organizing or planning political action (*CIDOC Catalog*, 1972, p. 2).

In the spring of 1961, Illich traveled through South America looking for a place to establish his institute. He decided upon Cuernavaca, Mexico, because of its climate and proximity to North America, but more importantly because of the liberal Sergio Mendez Arceo, Bishop of Cuernavaca. The new center had the support of the American bishops and of Fordham University. It was first called Center of Intercultural Formation (CIF), and later called Center of Intercultural Documentation (CIDOC).

Illich's purpose in establishing the center was ostensibly to help train missioners for Latin America. The Roman Catholic

Church in the United States had been requested by church authorities in Rome to send 10 percent of its personnel—about 20,000 persons—to Latin America. Illich's real purpose, however, was to keep all but the most progressive missioners out of Latin America. He was actually opposed to the church's program, but he undertook the task to minimize the harm that uninformed missioners might do in Latin America (Illich, 1969, pp. 53–54). Illich's program consisted of a strenuous emphasis on de-Yankeefication (Gray, 1969, p. 252). This emphasis consisted in rigorous training in the languages of Latin America, living a poor and meager existence in Cuernavaca, and especially confronting the radical views of Illich and others at the center.

By 1968 Illich's relationship with church authorities had begun to deteriorate. He had written an article in *America* magazine (Illich, 1967), a national Catholic weekly, rejoicing over the failure of the plan to send missioners to Latin America and calling for its immediate discontinuation. He criticized the plan as part of the effort of the West to keep Latin America within its own particular ideology. For him, the influx of United States missioners coincided with and baptized the Alliance for Progress and CIA projects. Illich further saw the coming of missioners and the investment of North American funds in the church of Latin America as an obstacle in the way of true church reform. These prevented the development of Latin-American solutions to its own problems.

Illich's and CIDOC's affiliation with the church ended in 1969. He had come under increasingly heavy attack also by conservatives in the Mexican hierarchy. He was once physically attacked while delivering a lecture at the National University in Mexico. Articles appeared in the press denouncing him as an atheist, Communist, and apostate. The Mexican bishops tried to get Cardinal Spellman to remove Illich from Cuernavaca, but the cardinal acted as Illich's protector. With Spellman's death, Illich's enemies moved quickly. Catholics were banned from attending the center. Illich was called to

Rome to answer charges. He went but refused to answer the questions. He made the whole matter public and resigned from his priestly office (Occampo, 1969).

Though CIDOC has no direct affiliation with the Roman Catholic Church, religious concerns remain prominent at the center. Sondeos, a series of book-length inquiries into the study of religious phenomenology in Latin America are still available from the center, as are texts of church councils and synods of Latin America. Its offering of courses concerned with religious problems and issues is being phased out. Illich continues to give lectures to church groups on religious topics. CIDOC, furthermore, still attracts a number of church-oriented persons to its language school and its classes.

A CIDOC catalog in 1973 described the center as "a meetingplace for persons whose common concern is the reconstruction of society and the understanding of the effects of social and ideological change on the minds and hearts of men" (p. 2). The center became known to North American educators because of the Seminar on Alternatives in Education held there during 1969–1970. Illich directed this seminar with Everett Reimer, whom Illich had known from his days in Puerto Rico.

While in Puerto Rico, Reimer and Illich frequently discussed the problems of the churches and the schools. Reimer was at that time secretary of the Committee on Human Resources of the commonwealth government. His chief concern in Puerto Rico was with the high dropout rates from the schools. These, he thought, would have to decline if the manpower needs of the commonwealth were to be met. Illich and Reimer both came to the conclusion that Puerto Rico and the countries of Latin America needed education but could not afford schools. It was for this reason that they began the Seminar on Alternatives in Education (personal interview with Ivan Illich, June 1972).

The seminar drew a number of educators from throughout the world. Paul Goodman, Paulo Freire, John Holt, Didier Piveteau, Joel Spring, and George Dennison were among the many who attended the weekly sessions. Two versions of the conclusions reached by the seminar exist in print. Illich wrote various articles which have been incorporated into *Deschooling Society* (1970). Reimer has published his own version of the conclusions in *School Is Dead* (1971). CIDOC has published all the papers relating to the seminar, compiled in four volumes (Catalog of Publications, 1973).

Illich has conducted a second seminar somewhat related to the Alternatives seminar, entitled "The Political Statement of Limits to Growth." In this seminar Illich is extending the argument used in *Deschooling Society* to other institutions of society. A book on this topic, *Tools for Conviviality* (Illich, 1973b), was the focus of analysis for the seminar. The center held a consultation in 1975 on the general theme of the multiple and independent limits to the further expansion of the industrial mode of production. Out of this seminar have come two additional books by Illich, *Energy and Equity* (1974) and *Medical Nemesis* (1975).

Though Illich's present concerns are not directed toward schooling, a knowledge of his present ideas is important for seeing more clearly his argument against schools. His critique and rejection of schooling as a proper form of education was based not so much on its failures as an institution as on its critical position in maintaining modern overindustrialized and overconsumerized society. Illich's social criticism becomes more evident in these latter concerns than it was in his analysis of the institutionalization of schooling.

Sources of Their Thought

In comparing and evaluating Illich and Freire, an important task is to delineate the respective sources of their thought. In the case of Freire, this is in some ways an easy task. He constantly supplies footnotes and quotations throughout his writings. It is easy to determine the various persons who have influenced the development of his thinking. In reading Freire, one gets the impression that his system is highly eclectic. He documents just about every important idea that he presents.

The difficulty in treating Freire's thought comes not in determining its sources, but in the area of finding consistency of structure. He draws on so many diverse thinkers that one begins to question how well these ideas are integrated. He quotes from the writings of religious thinkers, existential phenomenologists, Marxist theorists, and active revolutionaries. The net result of this marshaling of myriad sources is a confusion as to just what is the philosophy of Paulo Freire. As will be shown later, certain inconsistencies in his thinking are to be found.

Examining Illich at the level of sources is another task altogether. As Maxine Greene (1972) points out, he seems unaware of all writings in educational and social reform that preceded his own. Only rarely does he refer to sources. In the introduction to *Deschooling Society* (1970), Illich does mention his indebtedness to Everett Reimer and to a number of other thinkers, especially those who participated in the weekly seminars at CIDOC. But just where he has been influenced by others is rarely made clear in his writings.

Though there is some justification for this criticism leveled at Illich by Greene and others, a more careful examination of his writings does reveal a number of important influences upon him. In this regard, a recent bibliography which Illich (1972d) prepared for the CIDOC Seminar on Limits to Growth is most helpful. In *Medical Nemesis* (1975), Illich for the first time provides extensive references.

Freire's Religious Vision

A chief source and inspiration of the thought of both Freire and Illich is the religious tradition and theological writings which have formed both men. A major purpose of this book is an attempt to show that the religious dimension of their thought is perhaps the most important factor in understanding their social and educational thought. At all the major junctures of their thought, the religious dimension becomes most apparent and most influential. This religious dimension will be shown to be a most fruitful means for comparing and contrasting the ideas of Freire and Illich.

Freire was raised as a Catholic in Recife. One sees in his writings certain elements of Thomistic philosophy and theology. His static view of man and nature and his tired distinction between man and animals represent the philosophy of Thomas Aquinas. Most readers tend to ignore this part of Freire's thought, not understanding the tradition out of which he writes. Man and nature are presented by Freire as predetermined and given. Another key concept of Freire's is "speaking the Word." This has deep roots in the Judeo-Christian tradition through the Greek fathers, John's Gospel, and the Hebrew Wisdom Literature.

Traditional religion is not the only source for Freire's ideas. He also draws on more contemporary religious thinkers. Religious existentialists have greatly influenced him. When he speaks of dialogue and freedom, he echoes the words of Martin Buber and Gabriel Marcel. His key concept of "limit situation" is drawn from the German existentialist Karl Jaspers.

More recent theological trends in Latin America are even more influential. A theology of liberation has developed there which attempts to cast religion in the role of liberating man and societal institutions from oppressive elements. Theologians of this persuasion are keenly aware of the role that religion has played in Latin-American countries in maintaining the existing oppressive political and social institutions. They have begun to draw on certain elements in the Hebrew and Christian tradition that point to a more liberating role for religion.

Freire has both influenced and been influenced by these theological developments. His ideas on the liberating force of educational dialogue are paralleled by emphasis on the liberating force of religious activity. Freire continues to maintain connection with activist religious groups. He has on a number of occasions addressed religious audiences on the religious dimension of his thought.

The central religious problem is defining man's relationship to a transcendent being. Freire affirms God and speaks of man's relationship to him as central to his view of man and the world. The relationship that man should have with others and the relationships that should exist in society are determined by and modeled after the relationship that man has to his Creator. Domination and oppression should not exist among men, because this would not be true to what man is by reason of his relationship to his Creator. Freire (1969) speaks in this way of this relationship:

> His transcendence over us is based on the fact of our finitude and our knowledge of this finitude. For man is an incomplete being, and the completion of his incompleteness is encountered in his relationship with his Creator, a relationship which, by its very nature, can never be a relationship of domination or domestication, but is always a relationship of liberation. Thus religion (religare—to bind) which incarnates this transcendent relationship among men should never be an instrument of alienation. Precisely because he is a finite and indigent being, in this transcendence through love, man has his return to his source, who liberates him. (P. 15.)

Freire's religious views will be presented in various places in this work. The essential elements in his religious vision include the following: a view of God as actively involved in man's development and in the course of historical events; a view of Jesus as a radical reformer who calls men to a life of freedom and love; a view of the church as an institution which is actively involved in opposing oppression wherever it exists; a view of the Christian task as the effort to realize oneself in freedom and at the same time to work with God and fellow Christians against oppression.

Illich's Religious Vision

If Freire's religious vision of man and the world are an important dimension of his thought, it is also clear that Illich's religious vision and outlook are even more central to his social and educational criticism. Though he has formally resigned from the Roman Catholic priesthood, and though some of his later writings utilize less explicit religious language, Illich remains the priest and theologian. He is a religious reformer along the lines of Bernard of Clairvaux, who railed against the evil deeds of churchmen and societal leaders from the confines of his monastic surroundings. Like Bernard, Illich calls the church and then all of society away from its all too human failings to the new life which is the Kingdom of God. Like medieval reformers, he has established a form of life and an institution which is a presage of the future age.

During the years of his priestly ministry Illich's concern was directed toward the reform of the Roman Catholic Church. He has severely criticized the American church for its smugness, bureaucracy, and chauvinism. He called the clerical leaders of the North American church ecclesiastical conquistadores. He has argued against the cultural superiority of the church as if it were original sin. He has attacked the arrogance entailed in the missionary efforts which were used to domesticate the Puerto Rican immigrants in New York. His experience in Latin America has convinced him that similar methods were being used by the church to keep whole nations in a state of subservience. He has opposed a change in the rule of celibacy of the clergy, because it would stand in the way of the necessary declericalization of the church which is necessary to permit many lay persons to assume their rightful role in church communities. The church of the future that Illich envisages is a more familial type of church; it consists of small communities of interested persons pursuing common tasks through common efforts. What is preventing authentic religious life from taking place is the bureaucratization of the church and the existence of a class of professional churchmen.

Though an intrepid church reformer, Illich has always considered himself radically traditional and orthodox in his theological views. He is able to call the church to reform and engage in radical doubt concerning the institution of the church because of the certainties he maintains as a part of his religious vision. He believes in a transcendent God who controls the events of history, in the divinity of Christ, and in his continued presence in the Christian church through its duly established leaders and its liturgical institutions. He believes in transcendent meaning in all human life. He trusts that all of life, if left unhampered, would progress toward the Kingdom of God. These certainties enable him to call into question in a radical manner many aspects of the church as it exists. It is because of these certainties that he can be confident that men could build a new church and a new world.

Illich's religious view combines both prophetic and mystical dimensions. He is prophetic in calling churchmen back to the fundamentals of Christian faith. He is prophetic in his scathing criticism of the institutions of the church. He is prophetic also in his call to Christians to work with all men for the betterment of society.

The mystical impulse is also found in Illich. He speaks of man's intimate relationship with God, which has no need for a mediator. Illich is known to spend nights in prayer and meditation. He is deeply interested in the mystical traditions of the great religions of the world. A collection of Illich's writings (1971b) is devoted to his views on the mystical dimension of religion.

In *Deschooling Society* (1970) and later writings, Illich remains the religious reformer. But now he applies his efforts to the reform of the world and more particularly and essentially to the unmasking of the school as the central institution in maintaining society in its present condition. CIDOC is the secular monastery out of which he issues his reform tracts. It is also the model of what human institutions should become if they are truly to serve human purposes. His criticisms are directed at large industrialized nations, most especially the United States. He calls for the breakdown of bureaucracies. He heralds the necessary deprofessionalization of schooling, medicine, law, social service. He calls for the establishment of a convivial society in which convivial institutions will serve not themselves but the needs of the people (Illich, 1973b, pp. 10–12). Illich (1974) has also offered a critique of the modern transportation industry. In *Medical Nemesis* (1975) he has further developed his critique of the medical profession and health delivery systems.

Illich is able to engage in this radical doubt and criticism because of certainties in his religious vision. His vision convinces him that there are forces operative in man and in the world, both human and superhuman, and that these forces if unleashed can be trusted to build new institutions and a new world. What prevents the emergence of these new forms is the excessive bureaucratization of life, professional classes that exist to be served, thus preventing people from forming the types of communities that would better respond to their needs.

Illich's writings, again and again, use the example of religion to illustrate the process of developments he advocates for society. The cultural revolution, the deschooling process, is likened to the disestablishment of the church in the Western world. To many, these religious examples may appear to be useless relics from Illich's church days and consequently not to be taken seriously. But these constant comparisons of school to church, teacher to priest, schooling to salvation, certification to grace are controlling elements in his thought. Illich remains the reformer with the religious vision. The reform efforts are now, however, directed to other institutions in society.

Both Illich and Freire, then, can adequately be described as religious reformers. The religious vision that each man possesses has influenced greatly his view of man, society, the means of changing society, and educational criticisms and theories. Differences in religious visions also account for some of the important contrasts between these two contemporary Christians. In succeeding chapters I will develop the thought of each reformer and show how this has been influenced by his religious vision.

2
Christian Humanists

Both Freire and Illich are deeply religious, and these commitments have shaped their thought. The homes from which they came, their experiences in Catholic reform circles, and the particular theological or religious world view which they share powerfully influenced their careers. The type of religious view which they profess may adequately be described as Christian humanism. Freire sees the relationship between man and a transcendent Being as the norm for judging the relationship that should exist between man and man. This view is not new in Christian thought, but in Freire's thought it assumes great importance. It is at the basis of his view of man and of his revolutionary pedagogy. Illich goes about his work as one who is attempting to reform both man and society. His efforts to reform society are an extension of the reform efforts he directed against the Roman Catholic Church. Though he still appears interested in the reform of the church, he does not function in the official capacity of a minister within this church. His major reform efforts, therefore, are directed toward other institutions in society.

The purpose of this present chapter is to examine the humanistic dimension in the thought of Freire and Illich. Both men contend that they are Christian humanists. Illich himself has said that it is at this level that he can best be compared with Freire (Illich, private interview, June 1972). In many of their writings, both men appeal to a concept of human nature by which their educational and social goals are to be evaluated. Illich devotes the last chapter of *Deschooling Society* (1970) to his image of man, an image which he terms "Epimethean" (pp. 105–116). Freire terms "true humanization" as the goal of education for liberation. Thus a comparison of the thought of each thinker at this level, together with a criticism of this thought, will be most important in the overall attempt at comparison and evaluation.

An educator or social critic's view of human nature is crucial to his thought. However, appeals to human nature have to be carefully examined. One way to assert that something is good or true without having to make any argument for it is to assert that it is according to human nature. McClellan (1968, p. 250) has argued convincingly that an appeal to human nature is not an appeal to reasons or to arguments, but rather a decision to discontinue giving explanations and justifications. Therefore, in determining what a thinker means by human nature or in what his humanism consists, we arrive at the fundamental assumptions of his thought.

When Freire and Illich speak of human nature, they do so in most optimistic terms. Although they criticize the many evil things men have done to one another, they are still optimistic about man's potential for doing good. The statements that both men make are most idealistic about the future possibilities of mankind, though they are most critical in their judgments of the concrete things that men have done in the past and are doing in the present.

Illich's View of Human Nature

Erich Fromm (1969, p. 8) classifies Illich's philosophical position as one of radical humanism. Illich engages in radical doubt about everything. He critically questions all assumptions and institutions. This radical questioning is humanist because it is guided by Illich's view of what is best for man. "Humanist radicalism questions every idea and every institution from the standpoint of whether it helps or hinders man's capacity for greater aliveness and joy" (Fromm, 1969, p. 9).

The starting point of Illich's philosophy of man is the fact that man's existence is the realization of some superhuman plan, external to man. Illich's humanism thus is derived from innate human nature as this is interpreted by religious principles. As Schaff (1963, pp. 107–108) indicates, every era has its own definition of humanism. It is possible to speak of ancient humanism, of the humanism of early Christianity, of the Renaissance, the Reformation, the Enlightenment, and socialist humanism. Illich's humanism is religious. Man is a creature of God who has a continuing relationship with God. Man possesses freedom and dignity by virtue of this relationship. The task of man is to become the person he already is by virtue of the very being which God has given him. Pratte (1973, pp. 100–102) alludes to this religious humanism of Illich, but fails to develop its crucial impact in Illich's thought.

Freire's philosophic position may also be termed one of radical Christian humanism. He espouses the same Christian philosophy of man as Illich does. For Freire, man is free to become through his actions what he is already by virtue of his God-given essence. One finds in his writings the same radical doubt and questioning. He questions the existing relationships between rulers and ruled in society, between teachers and students. His doubt does not appear to be carried to the same length as Illich's; however, in an interview (Freire, 1970f, p. 15), he spoke favorably of Illich's view on the radical deschooling of society. Also, the humanist element is certainly present in his philosophic position. Freire (1970a) emphasizes the "humanist option in education" (p. 4), the humanization of man, and its educational implications. The humanist option for Freire is the liberating one. Humanization or liberation is for him the goal of political education and political activity.

Illich's image of man is presented in rather poetic terms in the last chapter of *Deschooling Society* (1970). He envisions the birth of Epimethean man and the demise of Promethean man. Promethean man forges institutions to correct the ills of man. He relies on results that are planned and controlled by man. The satisfaction he seeks is from a predictable process. It is this man that builds the rational and authoritarian society. This man makes his environment and then finds that he must constantly remake himself to fit it. The institutions that he makes end up being his master. Promethean man is the man of law, of science, of the machine, and of the computer. Illich's description of man is idealistic. Although Illich speaks in poetic terms of two different types of men, it is clear that he is referring in this manner to two qualities which exist in all men.

Illich expects the Epimethean nature of man to reemerge. This emergence can be neither planned nor produced. Epimethean man is the man of hope; he possesses a trusting faith in the goodness of nature and the human person. He values hope above expectations and loves people more than products. Illich's Epimethean man bears many resemblances to the Dionysian man forecast by Nietzsche in the nineteenth century. He is more like primitive man, who was initiated into society through mythical participation in sacred rites. Man must change things; he must stop remaking himself to fit his environment. We need less reliance on institutional process and more dependence on personal goodwill.

The complete description of Epimethean man must be filled out through other descriptions of man that we find in other passages in Illich's writings. The point of view is that of the classical liberal humanist. Man's freedom is at the core of this vision of man. Illich (1969) tells us that "each change in man's behavior results from his personal insight" (p. 145). In *Retooling Society,* Illich (1973a, pp. 3–23) argues that human survival is dependent on establishing procedures that permit ordinary people to recognize limits and to opt for survival in freedom.

One aspect of human freedom that is essential to Illich's thought is the freedom to learn. In an article written after *Deschooling Society,* Illich (1971a) points out the dangers of an uncritical disestablishment of the schools. He has also op-

posed certain radical reforms of schooling, such as development of free schools or the use of the voucher system, because these reforms perpetuate the existence of schools. Another fundamental problem he sees with these approaches is
that they do no justice to the basic concepts of learning and
of knowledge with their relationship to the freedom of man.
Illich believes

> that only actual participation constitutes socially valu-
> able learning, a participation by the learner in every
> stage of the learning process, including not only a free
> choice of what is to be learned and how it is to be
> learned but also a free determination by each learner
> of his own reason for living and learning—the part that
> his knowledge is to play in his life. (Illich, 1971a, p. 10.)

Illich's concept of freedom places him in the tradition of
Rousseau, nineteenth-century libertarians, and more contemporary educational reformers such as Paul Goodman.
This concept of free learning is basic to his thought and will
be examined later in this book.

Illich's philosophy of man demands, in the second place,
that men should be treated equally in society. However, Illich nowhere treats the problem of how equality of treatment is distinguished from sameness of treatment (Komisar
and Coombs, 1965). Illich tells us that "schooling opposes this
radical equality because of its selective and elitist nature"
(Illich, 1969, p. 115). The equality theme is quite pronounced
in *Deschooling Society* (1970) and in other writings. In his
most recent statements, this emphasis upon equality has led
him to espouse socialism and the ideals of socialist justice.
Illich (1973b) envisages

> the evolution of a life style and of a political system
> which give priority to the protection, the maximum use,
> and the enjoyment of the one resource that is almost
> equally distributed among all people: personal energy
> under personal control. (Pp. 11–12.)

Personal responsibility is a third aspect of human nature that he emphasizes. He speaks often of the need for persons to take more responsibility for their lives. Persons must reassume for themselves the responsibilities that they have given to the various institutions of society, such as schools, hospitals, courts, and churches. The convivial society that Illich sees emerging is one in which men will take autonomous control over all the tools of society. "One's access to the goods of society is to be limited only by another's equal freedom to utilize these goods" (Illich, 1973a, pp. 2–4).

Close personal relationships and interactions are the styles of human life most favored in Illich's future society (1969, p. 82). When speaking about the church of the future, Illich presents as a goal the face-to-face meeting of families around a table. He thus favors small communal types of organizations. His center at Cuernavaca is a place where people are trained to feel with others what change means to the heart. It is a place where close intimate relationships are fostered. The only institutions Illich favors are those in which technology is used to serve personal, creative, and autonomous interaction among men. The criteria by which all institutions are to be judged is their capacity to foster human development through the greatest amount of interaction as Illich argues in *Tools for Conviviality* (1973b, p. 13).

Illich's image of man entails a transcendent relationship to God as revealed in the person of Jesus Christ. Illich's belief in the religious dimension of man is most evident in his earliest writings collected in *Celebration of Awareness* (1969). His later writings do not present this image explicitly, but the impact of the religious dimension is no less present. This religious vision is one of hope and trust in man. In some ways it is a Protestant view of man's relationship to God, insofar as there is almost no need for intermediaries between man and God. In other ways, it is a liberal view with less emphasis on the doctrine of original sin. One could almost term his view of man Pelagian, an early Christian heresy which extolled man's power and free will at the expense of God's power to control man's life.

The Christian gospel is viewed by Illich as the power of God liberating man through the example of the person Jesus. This view of the gospel has often been emphasized by liberal and reformist thinkers. Jesus, the man who freed others, is presented as the ideal man whom all men should emulate. Jesus is presented as the one who offers judgment on the institutions of man and calls men to a more direct and intimate relationship with God. Illich's view of the Christian gospel is expounded in various chapters of *Celebration of Awareness* (1969, Chapters 4–7). Illich's theological vision is similar to that of certain Latin-American theologians of liberation (Alves, 1969; Gutiérrez, 1971).

Although Illich's image of man finds its counterpart in the writings of secular libertarians, the image must be seen as basically religious. Broudy (1972) misses this religious dimension in Illich's humanism. Illich is to be most clearly seen as a religious reformer. His image of man is drawn primarily from a particular reading of the Christian gospel and reinforced by a long tradition of Christian humanism. His view of human freedom owes more to Paul of Tarsus and Erasmus of Rotterdam than to Rousseau. This is so because he views this freedom as coming from man's transcendent relationship to God. His Epimethean image of man appears most inspired by Christian descriptions of future life. His emphasis on hope finds strong relationships to a concurrent development in theological circles toward a theology of hope, which emphasizes man's freedom and power to break down existing forms of life and to create newer ones more responsive to true human needs and nature. Illich's emphasis on hope in its theological dimensions finds its strongest parallel in the work of the theologian Jürgen Moltmann (1967). There are also similarities between Illich's thought and the more secular thought of Fromm (1968) and Bloch (1959).

Freire's View of Human Nature

Like Illich, Freire may rightly be regarded as a Christian humanist. He calls himself a humanist and refers to his philosophy and method as humanistic. He constantly refers throughout his writings (e.g., 1970b, pp. 5–6) to the vision of man that is at the basis of his thought. Humanization is for Freire the goal of every enterprise in which man is involved. Dehumanization, for Freire, describes every action that is destructive of true human nature and dignity. This obviously vague and almost tautological description represents the style that often characterizes Freire's writing. One of Freire's basic objections to the primers that were in use in Brazil centers on the vision of man that these primers imply. This view sees man as a passive being who is not responsible for making choices about his own education. Freire's clearest description of his pedagogical theory is presented in these words:

> Our pedagogy cannot do without a vision of man and of the world. It formulates a scientific humanist conception which finds its expression in a dialogical praxis in which teachers and learners, together, in the act of analyzing a dehumanizing reality, denounce it while announcing its transformation in the name of the liberation of man. (Freire, 1970b, p. 20.)

Other parts of this description will be analyzed later, but the passage brings out the humanist view that Freire takes of his work.

It has been indicated in Chapter 1 that the principal roots for the thought of Freire are Christian and Catholic. This is most evident in his view of man. Though he utilizes various traditions in developing his vision of man, the controlling concepts are religious. Man is essentially defined by his relationship to God, who has given him the powers of reflective and free choice. He is a being of relationships, first of all to God, and secondarily to his fellowman. Growing through these relationships, he becomes the person that he is destined to be. For Freire, man must struggle to become what he already is by virtue of the essence he has been given by God. For Freire, man's nature is incomplete and completion is to be found in a relationship to God (1969, p. 15). In this relationship, God gives man's nature a transcendental character. It is this striving for completeness that enables man to go beyond the limit situations in which he finds himself. As will be seen, Freire extends this capacity for transcendence from individuals to societies. Society's power to transcend itself finds its basis in "man's ontological and historical vocation to be more fully human" (Freire, 1970a, p. 40).

One recurrent theme in Freire's thought, which American readers tend to ignore or pass over lightly, is the extended comparison that he makes between men and animals. The comparison is explicit in just about everything that he writes, while nothing of this kind appears in the writings of Illich. Freire is constantly contrasting the reflection and freedom of men to the nonreflective and determined existence of animals. In making these comparisons, Freire draws for the most part on scholastic and existential categories. The vision of human nature that he espouses is brought out in these comparisons. Man is conscious of his own existence. He lives not only in an oppressive present but in past, present, and future. He enters into relationships with others. He develops a culture. He is able to take risks.

Though many tend to ignore this theme in Freire's writing, he contends that it is important and constantly reiterates it (Freire, 1969, p. 17; 1970a, pp. 87–90; 1970b, pp. 28–32; 1970c, pp. 1/4–1/9). It was this distinction that formed the basis of the preliminary sessions in his literacy programs. Freire considered the unreflective level of existence of many peasants in the northeast of Brazil to be close to the level of animal existence. He saw the same oppressive present as determining their lives. In these first sessions, Freire attempted to bring the participants to an awareness of the distinction between nature and culture. Nature was the condition of animals, who are determined to repeat again and again the same actions. Man, however, has a culture. He reflects upon what he does; he can do things differently. Freire used many illustrations in this stage of his method. They were used to motivate and raise consciousness. The illustrations are designed to bring out man's nature as a being who enters into relationships with others, engages in dialogue with others, forms particular cultures, invents better techniques and instruments, transforms nature by his work, and reflects upon his developing culture (Freire, 1973a, pp. 61–84). Freire made use of these illustrations only in Brazil, not in Chile. He found that the Chileans were more anxious to get immediately to the practical task of reading and writing.

One criticism can be made of Freire at this point. He takes no account whatsoever of attempts to show a continuity in nature between men and animals. In this area, Freire betrays his dependence upon scholastic philosophy and theology. Men and animals are placed at opposite poles. No mention is made of similarities that exist between men and animals. The revolution in biology ushered in by Darwin goes unnoticed in Freire's pages. He takes no account of the attempts of behaviorists and other psychologists to show the extent to which man's behavior is determined. One gets the impression from reading Freire that human and societal change can occur simply by willing it. This criticism can also be made of Illich in his exaggerated claims for human freedom and in his refusal to take into account the many factors that determine human choice.

Freire's religious humanism lies at the basis of this problem. This vision dictates that man's nature is essentially different from that of lower animals. The rigid categories of scholasticism and contemporary existentialism seem incapable of taking into account the biological and psychological findings of the past century. Or, more truthfully, these categories as used by Freire are incapable of this task. Some contemporary neo-Thomists, such as Bernard Lonergan (1957), make a serious effort to reconcile scholastic categories with the scientific tradition. One finds in no extant writing of Freire even an awareness of the problems that the work of Skinner (1971) and other behaviorists poses to his view of man and the world.

This criticism of Freire is not, as it might appear to be, a minor one. It is the contention of the author that Freire's faulty view of human nature (faulty insofar as he fails to take into account the limitations of human freedom) gives rise to an overly optimistic and simplistic view of the possibility of social and political change. He speaks of this change as if it were merely a matter of seeing its necessity and then willing its existence. At times, Freire comes through as the religious preacher, urging men to live better lives without showing them how to cope with the personal and societal obstacles that make the living of this life very difficult, if not impossible. Though Freire shows some awareness of the psychological obstacles to human freedom in his reference to Fromm's *Escape from Freedom,* more often he ignores this dimension and does not consider the many other limitations to freedom of action that are present in man's existence.

It can be said, then, that Illich and Freire share the same basic vision of man, the same basic concept of what it means to be human. Man is that being who is rational, self-conscious, free, and transcendent. Freire does develop this vision in more detail than does Illich. Freire is more concerned with establishing a definite philosophical position on human nature than is Illich. He connects himself explicitly with the classical Christian and humanist position.

This vision of man plays an important role in the thinking of both men. Many of their fundamental assumptions are included under the rubric of human nature. Their radicalism consists of calling all institutions in society and all human activities into question on the basis of whether or not they foster what they term true humanization (Freire) or promote the birth of Epimethean man (Illich). Their fundamental criticisms of the schools and of education depend upon this concept of human nature as the criterion of judgment. Their proposals for a liberating education and for education in a convivial society are consonant with the view of human nature that they espouse. Their hope for a revolution in society rests in their belief in certain attributes of man that they deem essential. Since the fundamental assumptions of both thinkers lie in this area of their thought, an evaluation of these assumptions goes to the very heart of their educational, social, and political philosophy.

Critique of Freire's and Illich's Views of Human Nature

A criticism of the Christian humanism propounded by Freire and Illich may be couched in religious terms, though the criticism could be made also in more secular language. Religious language is appropriate because both thinkers clearly place themselves in the Christian tradition. In their concept of man there is little recognition of original sin, the problem of human evil, and the sense of the tragic in human existence. Illich's Epimethean man, it appears, cannot will to do wrong. Freire's radical man will be able to act rationally, and in a nonoppressive manner. One gets the impression in reading Illich that, though man in the past has acted badly, it is possible for him to be totally different in the future; in fact, he sees a totally different man emerging. Freire writes as if he believes that the oppressed, once liberated, will be different persons. They will use their freedom wisely; they will not be exploitative.

In their criticisms of society, Illich and Freire certainly do point out the many evils that men perpetrate on their fellowmen. Freire describes the oppressive Brazilian society in which he labored for many years as an adult educator. Illich is aware of the evils that were perpetrated in Watts, Vietnam, and Latin America. Yet when both of them describe the man that will be, this man bears little resemblance to the man that is. This is no doubt the prerogative of utopian thinkers who proclaim the coming of the new man. It is no doubt the style and rhetoric of the preacher who proclaims the coming of the Kingdom. But it is a rather faulty base, not only for a criticism of society and its institutions, but also for a program of social and political revolution. The dark side of man will not be eliminated when the present oppressed are released and when men turn from manipulative to convivial institutions. Theories and programs of social change must deal realistically with this dark side of human nature. Precisely that is what Freire and Illich do not do in presenting their proposals for educational, social, and political change.

Both Illich and Freire seem to be involved in a contradiction. They contend that utopian or Epimethean man will emerge once man is released from oppressive restrictions. But who created these oppressive institutions in the first place? Illich admits the existence of the dark side of man when he speaks of Promethean man. Obviously this dimension of man was responsible for constructing oppressive institutions in the past. If he could do so then, why can he not do so once he is freed from present oppressive institutions? Freire too can be forced to admit that there must be a dark side of man that is responsible for present oppression. For otherwise he would have no adequate explanation for this oppression. Neither Freire nor Illich speaks of present institutions as mere stages in the development of man.

Utopian thinkers, like Freire and Illich, who do not posit stages of development are involved in a dilemma. If they admit the existence of present evil, they must admit the capacity of man to do evil and to fashion evil institutions. This capacity must be a part of man's nature. If they do not admit the existence of present evil, then their proposed utopia already exists. Freire and Illich certainly do not maintain this proposition.

It is not my contention that human nature is so corrupt that any possibility of change for the better is precluded. Pessimism is not being proposed as the alternative to the optimism of Illich and Freire. My assertion is that a complete vision of human nature demands thoughtful consideration of mountains of evidence that men do not spontaneously do what is considered good and just, once they are freed from certain restrictions. Giving persons an opportunity to be free is not necessarily a guarantee that they will act responsibly and humanely.

The vision of man espoused by Illich and Freire has been fashioned with dependence upon the religious tradition in which they were raised and educated. It is not, however, totally true to that tradition. It lacks some of the realism of that tradition with its strong insistence upon original sin or the corruptibility of man. It appears that these thinkers have stated as a present possibility for man what the tradition sees to be possible only in some future existence. Views such as those that Illich and Freire expound were often expressed within the tradition, usually by religious reformers who eventually attempted to put their views into practice in monasteries or sects. Utopian tendencies, though at times influential in broader communities, usually ran themselves out in smaller groups. It is interesting that both Freire and Illich have established small institutions where their utopian visions can find some expression.

The vision of man held by Illich and Freire is clearly identical to the vision of transcendent society propounded by utopian socialists. It possesses the same faith in the perfectibility of man once the deforming institutions of the past and present are removed. Some of the weaknesses of this vision have been pointed out by Heilbroner (1970). He tells us that the deepest weakness of that vision

> has been its failure to formulate a conception of human behavior in all its historical, sociological, sexual, and ideational complexity, a conception that would present

"man" as being at once biologic as well as social, tragic
as well as heroic, limited as well as plastic. (Heilbroner,
1970, p. 105.)

Events in modern socialist states have indicated that these
states must always live in fear of the secret "corruptibility"
of the people.

The view of man propounded by Illich and Freire has been
termed here as utopian. As will be seen, the entire thought
of Freire and Illich is cast in this mold. Utopian is not used
here in any pejorative sense. Utopianism as a very specific
type of orientation to social change has been discussed by
many scholars, including Mannheim (1936), Popper (1963)
and Kolakowski (1968). These scholars show the utopian vision as a necessary part of the revolutionary vision. Kolakowski (1968) speaks of utopia as

> the striving for changes which "realistically" cannot be
> brought about by immediate action, which lie beyond
> the foreseeable future and defy planning. Still utopia is
> a tool of action upon reality and of planning social action.
> (Kolakowski, 1968, p. 70.)

Though Kolakowski does not specifically relate utopian social
thought to a utopian vision of man, there is a clear connection between the two. The belief that man can perfect society rests on the assumption that man himself is inherently
good and perfectible.

It is most difficult to argue against the utopian view of man
espoused by Illich and Freire because one is dealing here
with a matter of almost religious faith. Illich and Freire assert
that man is capable of being totally different from what he
has been in the past. For Illich, the birth of the new man,
Epimethean man, has already taken place and his numbers
are increasing. Nothing can be done to increase the rate of
his emergence; nothing can be done to decrease it. Men can
only celebrate this emergence. In rejecting this vision, one
has two options. Either man will always be as he has been or
he will be able to change for the worse and for the better,

both within limits. Faith in the latter seems to be better substantiated in the history of man.

The utopian vision of man has advantages and disadvantages. It has inspired reformers and revolutionaries to work for needed change in society. It has been a healthy counterbalance to the view that sees all change as impossible. It has enabled man to break out of present and past institutions. It has been the inspiration of political and social and religious revolutions.

The disadvantages of the vision have also been documented. The holding out of impossible goals has diverted people's attention from what can be realistically attempted. The far-off vision has blinded those who hold it to the proper and realistic assessment of present obstacles to the realization of the vision. Human experiments in utopian living have shown clearly that in a short time the new utopian man begins to resemble the man he is attempting to replace.

The utopian vision of man in Illich and Freire leads inevitably to utopian visions of social change and revolution. It is almost impossible to discuss the one without the others. There is a real sense, perhaps, in which one's vision of man and one's vision of society and one's vision of the possibility for change in society are one vision. Statements about man are not statements about some inner essence or being; they are rather statements about what man does or is capable of doing. Many persons today would prefer not to discuss such questions as visions of man and concepts of human nature. This type of language appears too transcendental and metaphysical. However, both Illich and Freire belong to a tradition of thought that expresses itself in such a manner. In speaking in this traditional mode Freire and Illich indicate their fundamental assumptions. In our grappling with the vision of man proposed by these two thinkers, we have found areas in which they can be compared and areas in which they can be criticized. The philosophy of man espoused by Freire and Illich leads to a second area of comparison—their social criticism.

3
Religious Social Critics

In his critique of *Deschooling Society,* Gintis (1972, p. 72) makes the point that Illich, unlike many other educational reformers, does not treat the system of schools as if it existed in a social vacuum. Illich views the internal irrationalities of modern education as reflections of the larger society. This same observation can also be made of Freire. His critique of traditional literacy methods used in Brazil and Chile is related to his analysis of the social systems that exist in those countries. Both men focus upon education and schooling because of their crucial role in maintaining the existing social structure. By the same token, schools are considered crucial instruments for establishing the new society that both Illich and Freire envision. Illich sees deschooling as the first task for the accomplishment of his cultural revolution. Freire views his libertarian education as the instrument for bringing people to awareness of the cultural contradictions in the existing social systems.

The social criticism in which both Freire and Illich engage is based in part, as was their vision of man, upon their theological visions and their experiences as members of the institutional church. It will be shown that Illich's criticism of social institutions is a continuation of his criticism of the church. He raises the same issues and uses the same types of arguments in both cases. Freire's social criticism is based on the perspective of the theology of liberation which is currently espoused among reform-minded Christians in Latin-American countries.

Illich's Critique of Society

Illich's social criticism essentially addresses the various institutions of society. He points out what he considers the evils of a present institution—for example, the school, church, or transportation. He then proceeds to propose some image of what should replace this institution. He describes briefly the means of bringing about the type of society that he envisions. Illich seems to believe that the same types of failings characterize all modern institutions, no matter in what country they are found. He views most modern institutions as manipulative and destructive of human freedom and happiness. The institutions and the society that he proposes are termed "convivial" (Illich, 1973b, xxiv). The convivial society is the society of the future, but there are certain elements of this society already in existence. In this society, tools or technology are utilized to promote the greater freedom of men. Most of Illich's writings (1972a, 1973a, 1973b, 1974, 1975) after *Deschooling Society* (1970) are concerned with the necessity of working for this society, a description of the institutions of this society, and a discussion of the political measures that must be taken to bring it about.

The first institution to which Illich directed his radical humanistic criticism was the church. For him, the church was the Roman Catholic Church in its local, national, and international organizational structure. This was the institution in which he was raised, in which he served as priest, and which he ardently wished to reform. He still considers himself a faithful member of this institution even though he has formally resigned from active ministry as a priest.

The types of criticisms that Illich makes of the church find parallels in the criticisms that he makes of all modern institutions. He has begun to make the long road through these various institutions. Illich's central concept (1973a), the institutionalization of values, which he sees taking place in all areas of society, is taken from Ellul's *The Technological Society* (1964). Illich's criticisms of the church are found in the various essays of *Celebration of Awareness* (1969). In *Deschooling Society* (1970) his church criticism has become the point of comparison for his criticism of the schools. What is involved here is more than mere analogy. Illich sees the same dynamics involved in the pathology of both institutions. In later writings (Illich, 1972a, 1973a, 1973b, 1974, 1975), it is Illich's criticism of the institutionalization of education that becomes the point of reference for his criticisms of medicine, social work, production, transportation, and law. Presently Illich is applying his critical insights to all institutions of society, both in the area of production and in the area of services. One sees then the same basic arguments throughout all of Illich's essays. The basis of his critical stance toward all institutions was developed in his criticisms of the church, and it is these criticisms that must now be examined.

Illich's Criticism of the Church. The church as an institution is primarily criticized for what it does to its members. It fails to respond to the particular needs of minority groups within it by imposing standard laws, practices, and teachings on all its members (Illich, 1969, pp. 31–40). It impedes the freedom of its people and ministers by insisting on clearly defined roles for both. It places a ministerial class between the people and God, thus alienating members from true religion. Its large bureaucratic organizations and services prevent face-to-face encounters, which are essential for true religion to develop. Through its bureaucratic arrangements, religion has become a commodity by which one achieves social status and is certified as worthy of salvation. Church policies prevent true equality among men by maintaining the present social class structure through collaboration with other institutions in society, especially political institutions. Illich (1969, pp. 53–68) contends that pouring more money into Latin America will not solve the problems of the church. What is necessary is radical change and restoration of the pastoral system.

Illich is most critical of overprofessionalization in the church. *Celebration of Awareness* (1969) includes the controversial essay "The Vanishing Clergyman," in which Illich calls for the dissolution of the priestly caste. This is the caste that presides over the church bureaucracy. This bureaucracy can be dismantled if laymen are permitted to perform the functions of the priest in society (Illich, 1969, p. 77). If a minister continues to work within the church institution, he should remain only to subvert it (Illich, 1969, p. 78). Men must be free to pursue their religious life without interference from the priests. He views the role of priest as an essential and legitimate function in the Christian community. But he asserts that in the present institution the priests block people from doing for themselves what they can and must do. The priestly ministry as it exists also does positive harm to people in their religious lives by keeping them docile and submissive. Illich does not define the functions of the priestly ministry in his church of the future. Neither does he adequately explain what it is that people would be able to do for themselves in his proposed church. This same lack of specifics will be found in Illich's treatment of the teacher-student relationship.

The institutional church is, for Illich, in serious trouble. People abandon it who are most needed for its continuance. The problem with the church is not so much with its members but "rather with the structure itself" (Illich, 1969, p. 72). The present structures developed as a response to past situations vastly different from the present situation. The present structure of priestly caste, large meetings of organizations, and mass-produced initiations work against the very purposes for which the institution was established.

Illich is most critical of the missionary efforts of the church, especially those directed at developing nations by the United States and other industrialized Western countries. In an article, "The Seamy Side of Charity" (Illich, 1969, pp. 53–68), which caused much controversy when it first appeared in 1967, Illich called missionary efforts "part of the many-faceted effort to keep Latin America within the ideologies of the West" (p. 58). These efforts have the effect of supporting the *status quo* in these countries by stifling necessary church reforms. Through such missionary efforts social control is effectively achieved. Thus the church is a partner in maintaining the existing class structure in these countries.

In various essays in *Celebration of Awareness* (1969), Illich draws a picture of the new church. It is to include "intimate familial celebrations of conversion to the gospel in the milieu of the home" (p. 63). The new church will be open to the possibilities of sacralizing all persons and all communities. Illich (1969) envisions that

> an adult layman, ordained to the ministry, will preside over the normal Christian community of the future. . . . The periodic meetings of friends will replace the Sunday assembly of strangers. The minister will be a man mature in Christian wisdom rather than a seminary graduate formed professionally through "theological formulae." I foresee the face-to-face meetings of families around a table rather than the impersonal attendance of a crowd around an altar. (Illich, 1969, p. 82.)

The priest will cease to be the authoritative figure he has been in the past. Church bureaucracy will come to an end. The church will no longer place its faith in efficient management but in the preaching of the gospel (Illich, 1969, p. 97).

"The Powerless Church" is an essay that gives further insights into his view of the church of the future (Illich, 1969, pp. 95–105). The essay states that the church should play no part in social change and development. The task of the church is to preach the gospel and to celebrate the experience of change that is taking place in the world. "The church teaches us to discover the transcendental meaning of this experience of life." (Illich, 1969, p. 99.) In the past the church has participated in social change either as a conservative or dynamic force:

> She has blessed governments and condemned them. She has justified systems and declared them as unholy. She has recommended thrift and bourgeois values and declared them anathema. We believe that the moment has come for the church to withdraw from specific social initiative. (Illich, 1969, p. 101.)

Social change, for Illich, should be left to other groups. The church should not compromise its commitment to transcendental values. As will be seen, the distinction that Illich makes between the church's political role and its commitment to transcendental values can be criticized on a number of grounds.

The first mention of education in Illich's writings concerns theological education in the Christian churches. His suggestions here presage his later radical views on education. Theological education should not merely prepare a person to assume an assigned role in church society, it should be deeply personal and experiential. This education is best received in small groups. Illich contends that much of what the future minister will need can be received from active life and experience in a Christian community. Illich calls for the closing of the seminary, the dethronement of the theology professor, and the extension of theological study to all members of the community, not just the select caste of priests (Illich, 1969, pp. 91–94).

One final aspect of Illich's church criticism concerns the question of implementing these reforms. Illich sees the deinstitutionalization of the church as already taking place. Many priests have abandoned the clerical state. Many who remain in the church work at goals counter to those of the institution. He sees some advances made through the Second Vatican Council. Illich's faith is in a transcendent power working through men to bring about the radical restructure of the church and the death of excessive ecclesiastical bureaucracy.

Illich (1969, p. 68) chides reformers for planning the new church rather than engaging in the search for the living church which is among us. Illich concludes his essay on "The Vanishing Clergyman" with a strong faith in a transcendent power to bring about the new church. In sermonlike language, he asserts that

> the Spirit, continually re-creating the church, can be trusted. Creatively present in each Christian celebration, He makes men conscious of the kingdom which lives in them. Whether composed of a few persons around the deacon, or of the Church's integral presence around the bishop, the Christian celebration renews the whole church, the whole of humanity. The church will clearly manifest the Christian faith as the progressively joyful expression of love's personal meaning—the same love which all men celebrate. (Illich, 1969, p. 94.)

The roots of Illich's criticism of the church lie in his conception of the proper understanding of the gospel, with its emphasis on simplicity, poverty, freedom, and love. Illich sees the gospel as opposed to professionalization, bureaucratization, and political involvement.

Illich's Criticism of the Schools. Since the latter 1960's, Illich has turned his attention from the church to a criticism of other institutions of society. The school system was next on his list. Illich first got interested in the problems of school systems through his association with Everett Reimer while both men were in Puerto Rico. Reimer, at that time, was investigating manpower problems in Puerto Rico and their relationship to school-leaving. Reimer (1971, p. 10) states that he and Illich found common interests in the problems of church and school. Over the past thirteen years, both men have investigated these problems in various seminars held at CIDOC.

Illich's first criticisms of the schools are found in two essays reprinted in *Celebration of Awareness* (1969). The first of these, "The Futility of Schooling in Latin America," appeared in *Saturday Review*. Illich contends that this article also "may help to demonstrate the general futility of world-wide education" (1969, p. 106). Illich contends that schooling is the cause of Latin America's problems and can in no way be part of the solution to these problems. Modern schooling for him is essentially an arm of American imperialism that produces rigid class structures, maintains social control, and effectively blocks equal educational opportunity.

Some of Illich's arguments against the institution of the church are found here. Through schooling, man's need for education has been rationalized into "an all-embracing persuasion, religion, or ideology" (Illich, 1969, p. 111). Illich had criticized the church for its institutionalization of true religious values. The product of the institutional church is salvation in an afterlife. The school promises temporal salvation as its main product. The school, like the church, effectively accomplishes control over the lives of the people and maintains the existing class structure. It prevents man from being truly free to pursue his own salvation (Illich, 1969, p. 112).

The extension of Illich's criticisms from the church to the school is found most explicitly in the commencement address he gave at the University of Puerto Rico. In "School: The Sacred Cow" (Illich, 1969, pp. 123–135) he calls for the disestablishment of the school just as the church has been disestablished in most modern states. Illich gives two main reasons for the necessity of this. First, school, like the church, prevents the achievement of genuine values because it prevents man from achieving these values for himself. Between man and this achievement a professional group has been placed that has a monopoly over the products of the institution. The scholastic rite, that is, attendance and graduation from school, initiates one into a community of consumers in a technological age. Secondly, the school, like the church, is supported by existing governments and does their bidding. It controls citizens; it maintains the existing social classes; it certifies the probity of individuals. Mother church, one, holy, catholic, and apostolic, has been replaced by alma mater, accredited, compulsory, untouchable, and universal. Faith in the church and the law of compulsory attendance at Mass has given way to faith in the school and compulsory school laws. Dropouts from both institutions are severely handicapped in society. Radical reformers of both institutions are accused of subversion, irreverence, and lunacy. The new school that Illich proposes resembles the new church in its respect for the freedom of the person and in its smallness. Illich compares the purposes of the new education with the purposes of the new church in this manner:

> The purpose of public education should be no less fundamental than the purpose of the church, although the purpose of the latter is more explicit. The basic purpose of public education should be to create a society in which society obliges each individual to take stock of himself and his poverty.

> Education implies a growth of an independent sense of life and a relatedness which go hand in hand with increased access to, and use of, memories stored in the human community. (Illich, 1969, p. 134.)

The true school, like the true church, is the place for encounter, for surprises. Hope for religious and educational salvation "lies in our being surprised by the Other" (Illich, 1969, p. 133). Illich sees the process of deschooling already taking place and urges his listeners, university graduates, to join in that work.

This essay, more than any other, shows the religious bent of Illich's thinking on society. He sees himself and other critics of the schools engaged in prophecy and charismatic activity. Theological insights about man, God, and human institutions are presented. There is trust in a transcendent power who works with man in history to accomplish what is right. The message is one of repentance, faith, hope, love, and perseverance to the end in spite of threats of martyrdom, persecution, and the stake (Illich, 1969, p. 129).

A more extensive analysis and evaluation of Illich's criticisms of the schools and his educational proposals will be found in later chapters. The purpose of this chapter is to show the religious inspiration for Illich's societal criticisms. To do this, it must be shown that these criticisms arise from the particular religious vision that Illich has of man and human society.

Illich's Criticism of Other Institutions of Society. In his earlier works, *Celebration of Awareness* (1969) and *Deschooling Society* (1970) Illich occasionally extends his criticisms beyond the church and school. In the essay "A Call to Celebration" (Illich, 1969, pp. 15–18), he issues the challenge to break the obsolete social and economic systems that divide our world between the overprivileged and the underprivileged. In another essay, "Violence: A Mirror for Americans" (Illich, 1969, pp. 19–28), he condemns the American system of government for resorting to planned violence in Watts, Vietnam, and Latin America. In the essay "Sexual Power and Political Potency" (Illich, 1969, pp. 95–104) he addresses the problem of overpopulation in society. His first detailed attack on the evils of industrial society is found in "Planned Poverty: The End Result of Technical Assistance" (Illich, 1969, pp. 157–175). He criticized the power of the institutions we have created in that they shape not only our preferences but also our sense of possibilities (Illich, 1969, p. 160). His criticism is directed chiefly against the Alliance for Progress, which he contends increases the sense of poverty in Latin America by creating demands for goods and services that are unnecessary for Latin Americans.

Deschooling Society (Illich, 1970) details at greater length Illich's criticisms of modern industrial society. He levels attacks against rigid class structures, unequal distribution of wealth, excessive bureaucracy, and a host of other evils. Illich's key arguments against modern society are directed against slavish adherence to the values of the consumer society. The institutions that men have formed in society have now begun to create a demand for unnecessary goods. Corporate bureaucracies have become autonomous and manipulative. Illich places the various institutions on a spectrum ranging from manipulative, which hook men on their products, to convivial, which guarantee men necessary human freedom and autonomy. Modern warfare, transportation systems, and schools are examples of the former. Telephone linkups, public markets, sewage systems, and the postal system are examples of the latter (Illich, 1970, pp. 52–64).

In his later writings Illich has turned more and more to the examination of various modern institutions and proposals for placing rational limits to the growth of all institutions. *Institutional Inversion* (1972a) contains essays on the institutionalization of health and law. The basic content of these essays is contained in *Retooling Society* (1973a) and *Tools for Conviviality* (1973b), *Energy and Equity* (1974), and *Medical Nemesis* (1975).

Illich's criticism of society remains a deeply religious one, even as he passes from the church and school to other institutions of society. The religious imagery is found throughout *Deschooling Society* (1970), it is explicit in a number of places in *Retooling Society* (1973a), it is implicit throughout all his writings.

Illich gave the most explicit expression of his religious criticism of society in a talk he delivered in Lima, Peru, in 1971 (Illich, 1972b). He contended that his message comes from the reading of the Scriptures and from a return to the purest tradition of the church. He announced "the coming of the Kingdom which is not of this earth: the Kingdom whose mystery we are privileged to know" (p. 47). Illich called for "an anti-technocratic consensus [which] easily translates into the need for voluntary poverty as it was preached by the Lord" (p. 48). Illich saw his message as consonant with the very heart of the Christian gospel:

> Self-chosen poverty, powerlessness, and nonviolence are
> at the heart of the Christian message. Because they are
> among its most tender elements, they are also among the
> most easily corrupted, ridiculed, and neglected. . . . The
> Christian message is also the most rational policy in a
> world increasingly devoted to widening the gap be-
> tween rich and poor. (Illich, 1972b, p. 48.)

Illich, the religious prophet and reformer, saw his effort to
set limits on progress, production, and consumption as a religious crusade to fashion a society in which men will be able
to develop as free creatures of God. He showed most clearly
the religious dimension of his entire work when he wrote:

> In the name of God we must denounce the idolatry of
> progress and the polluting escalation of production. We
> must expose the pseudo-theology of education as prepa-
> ration for a life of frustration consumption. We must
> remind men that God has created a good world and has
> given us the power to know and cherish it without the
> need of an intermediary. We know . . . that man grows
> up and learns in the measure in which he is engaged in
> personal, intimate—always surprising—intercourse with
> others in a meaningful environment, whereas he shrinks
> and shrivels when he is served by officials. Consequently,
> we must refuse to cooperate in any attempt to create a
> man-made environment in which the lives of all persons
> would depend on their having been clients of a service
> organization. (Illich, 1972b, p. 48.)

In this essay, Illich spells out the elements of the antitechnocratic consensus which the translation of the Christian
message into today's situation demands. Technology must be
snatched from the hands of the technocrats and placed in the
hands of the people. It calls for a world in which "radical
limits on consumption are arrived at by agreements among
a vast majority and ultimately in the interest of all" (1972b,
p. 48). All of this demands courage, to be sure; but God,
according to Illich, will not be found wanting.

In *Tools for Conviviality* (1973b), Illich puts this basically religious message into a more secular tone when he urges people to "learn to live within bounds."

> This cannot be taught. Survival depends on people learning fast what they cannot do. They must learn to abstain from unlimited progeny, consumption, and use. It is impossible to educate people for voluntary poverty or to manipulate them into self-control. It is impossible to teach joyful renunciation in a world totally structured for higher output and the illusion of declining costs. (Illich, 1973b, p. 65.)

Illich's call for voluntary poverty, chastity, and joyful renunciation of the present world underscores the basically religious dimension of the reforms he proposes. For Illich, it would appear, the gifts of poverty, chastity, and the spirit of renunciation would come from the spirit of God within man.

Freire's Criticism of Society

Paulo Freire, like Illich, places his criticisms of education within the structure of a criticism of all institutions of society. Freire also is greatly influenced by the religious vision he shares with Illich. Though both engage in social criticism, greatly influenced by their common religious vision, there are serious differences in the manner in which they view the religious tradition of which they are a part. Consequently, they differ at times on the particular criticisms they make of society, in their proposals for a new society, and in the means they propose to bring about the new society.

While Illich began his critique of social institutions by criticizing the church, Freire has come to this type of criticism only lately in his writings. In fact, one of the greatest weaknesses of his analysis of Brazilian society in *Education for Critical Consciousness* (1973a), which includes a translation of *Educação como prática da liberdade* (1967), is his failure to consider the role of the church in maintaining the existing level of political and social awareness among the people. One would never gather from reading Freire that the conservative Roman Catholic hierarchy was one of the forces opposing the reforms of the Goulart government in which Freire was deeply involved, as de Kadt (1970) has argued. Freire speaks only in general of "rightist forces" that opposed these reforms. His analysis never differentiates the various elements of oppression that existed in Brazilian society at that time. To be sure, Freire does, in *Education for Critical Consciousness* (1973a), point out certain false religious notions that operated in the consciousness of oppressed peoples. But nowhere in the work does he engage in the type of criticism of the church that pervades Illich's works and is called for in analyzing Brazilian society in the early 1960's. A comparison with Skidmore (1967) shows the weaknesses of Freire's analysis in this area.

Freire's Criticism of the Church. Since 1970, Freire has been an educational consultant with the World Council of Churches in Geneva. In this capacity, he has begun to criticize institutional religion more and more. This is done, however, in rather general terms and with little reference to specific countries and problems. In "The Educational Role of the Churches in Latin America" (1972a), Freire criticizes the churches for failing to exercise the true prophetic function which is theirs. He urges the churches to work actively against oppression, in whatever form it is found. The churches cannot be neutral, because neutrality means supporting the *status quo*. Examples of oppression are class-determined societies, oppressive power elites, and capitalism. The true gospel for Freire is prophetic, utopian, and revolutionary (Freire, 1972a, p. 11). It calls believers to work for change, revolution, and liberation. Jesus is presented as a person who worked for radical change. The religious revolutionary engages in living out the Passover or Easter through denouncing oppression and announcing liberation. Redemption is interpreted as the Christian's willingness to undergo death by struggling for new life and freedom for oppressed peoples.

Freire believes that he is calling the churches back to the true message of the gospel. His critique of the institutional church is clear here. In attempting to remain neutral in political struggles, it has supported the existing repressive regimes. The church has involved itself in bureaucratic paper-shuffling (Freire, 1972a, p. 3). It is "dying of cold in the warm bosom of the bourgeoisies" (Freire, 1972a, p. 9). He sees the modernizing efforts of the church as basically a conservative action, reforming only to maintain the *status quo.*

Freire's discussion of the religious person's participation in revolution seems to include an approval of the use of violent means to achieve revolutionary purposes. He speaks approvingly of those Christians who "recognize revolution as the road to liberation for the oppressed classes, and the military coup as a revolutionary option" (Freire, 1972a, p. 12). He also states:

> Today's Latin American Christians . . . will disagree at times, especially over the proper tactics to be used, but there are those who . . . commit themselves to the oppressed classes and stay firm in that position. . . . These individuals, some churchmen and some laymen, had to take their bruises and cuts during the transition so as to move on from an idealistic view of reality to a dialectical one. (Freire, 1972a, p. 12.)

Freire's view of the gospel and what it demands of Christians differs sharply here from Illich's. Illich sees commitment to the gospel as entailing standing above the political processes. The church is to renounce any temptation to become actively involved in political changes. The gospel that Illich wants preached is one of poverty, renunciation, and nonviolence. The church should be interested in changing men, not in changing societies, according to Illich (1969, p. 99). He admits that at times the church has participated in the shaping of social change. "She has blessed governments and condemned them. She has justified systems and declared them unholy" (Illich, 1969, p. 102). Illich contends that if the church in Latin America uses the power base it has in promoting social and political reforms, "then she perpetuates her inability to witness to that which is specific in her mission" (Illich, 1969, p. 103).

The difference between Illich and Freire on this point is striking. The difference might be explained by their differing experiences with church involvement in social and political change. Illich's views were formed in part by his connection with the Roman Catholic Church in Puerto Rico. It formed a political party in order to oppose the government's attempt to foster birth control in that country. Illich viewed this intrusion as harmful not only to the Commonwealth but also to the essential mission of the church. He was also critical of the missionary activity in Latin America, which seemed to coincide with the political ideology of the United States. So Illich was involved in what he considered detrimental incursions of the church into the political arena.

Freire on the other hand experienced what he considered the detrimental effects of nonintervention of the Latin-American churches in the struggles of oppressed peoples to achieve authentic liberation. In these instances nonintervention was for Freire tantamount to siding with the oppressors. Temperament and experience no doubt further explain the difference between these two men. Freire is by nature an activist who has always been involved in political struggles where the church is a crucial force in society. Illich sees religion in more spiritual or mystical terms.

The difference between Illich and Freire in their criticism of the church is important because it will shape their views of the type of revolution they propose for society and for the schools of society. Freire advocates political revolution as the means to true liberation. Illich contends that political revolutions have not brought about desired changes in the countries in which they have taken place. He advocates instead his particular form of cultural revolution.

To return to Freire's religious vision, the theological basis of his work has so impressed some scholars that they contend that his work is basically theological. Freire (1972b) asserts that he is not a theologian but is basically an educator. Most of his more recent writings indicate that he is becoming more and more theological in his thought. A number of recent dissertations (Grabowski, 1972, pp. 130–133) have assessed the theological nature of Freire's work. Our purpose is to show how his particular religious vision has influenced his criticism of society and his proposals for social reform. This issue of the theological nature of Freire's work is introduced merely to strengthen the contention that the social criticisms made by Freire are inspired at least in part by his particular theological vision.

Freire's work is most akin to what is termed secular theology, political theology, or theology of liberation. This type of theology is similar to the social gospel that developed in this country in the late nineteenth century in response to the general shock of urbanization and industrialization. The master motif of the social gospel was the coming of the Kingdom of God through the progressive growth of love in society. It emphasized social and political action at the expense of subjectivism, otherworldliness, and false apocalypticism. Harvey Cox (1965) reintroduced a form of this social gospel into the theological world in the 1960's by challenging the churches to join secular movements. For Cox such involvement constituted the essential mission of the church. Latin-American theologians have termed their social activity vision of Christianity a theology of liberation (Alves, 1969).

Fundamental to this type of religious vision and to the religious vision of Freire is a particular notion of God. The symbol of God presented is not the Unmoved Mover of Aristotle or the Subsistent Being of Aquinas. It is rather the active and dynamic God of the Hebrews and the human person of Jesus. God is someone who acts to save men. He is forever creating man and the world with man's cooperation. He delivers a people from bondage. Jesus is presented as the radical critic of oppressive institutions. In this view, the symbol of God as Savior refers not so much to individual salvation as to the process of bringing men and societies to true freedom. The task of the Christian is not to save his soul but to work with God in saving the world by combating all forms of human oppression. Original sin is given a social interpretation as referring to all forces of evil which man and God struggle against and which prevent true freedom. The resurrection and future life with God are concrete symbols of the new life that exists in a utopian future.

Freire's writings indicate that this interpretation of the God symbol is operative in his criticism of society and in his plan for the transformation of society. Freire (1969) presented God as a person who stands not for the domination of man but for his liberation. "Man's transcendent relationship is one in which man's freedom is guaranteed" (Freire, 1969, p. 15). In *Pedagogy of the Oppressed* (1970a), he attacked the "false view of God which fosters fatalism in oppressed peoples" (p. 162). This false view is based on the myth that rebellion is a sin against God (Freire, 1970a, p. 136). In "A Letter to a Theology Student," Freire (1972b) expressed the dynamic nature of the God symbol underlying his social criticism:

> The Word of God is inviting me to re-create the world, not for my brothers' domination but for their liberation. . . . The Word of God is not some content to be poured into us as if we were mere static recipients for it. And because it [the Word of God] saves, that Word also liberates, but men have to accept it historically. They must make themselves subjects, agents of their salvation and liberation. (Freire, 1972b, p. 7.)

In this letter, Freire relates his work explicitly to the theology of liberation or utopian theology currently being developed by theologians in Latin America:

> Theology has to take its starting point from anthropology. That is why I insist that a utopian and prophetic

theology leads naturally to a cultural action for liberation, and hence to conscientization. (Freire, 1972b, p. 8.)

This utopian and prophetic theology should begin with a new
notion of God as "a presence in history, [who] does not in the
slightest keep man from 'making history'—the history of his
liberation" (Freire, 1972b, p. 8).

Freire's Criticism of the Schools. Freire's criticisms of the
schools parallel those of Illich's, though Freire speaks more
about the process of education than he does about the effects
of the institution. Freire's interests have always been centered in adult education both at the literacy and the postliteracy levels. His works contain many criticisms of literacy
methods that are used in Latin-American countries. He
terms the educational procedure of these methods "domesticating," "nutritive," and "banking." Freire sees this type of
education as the root cause of the lack of proper development in Latin-American countries. His analysis of Brazilian
society in *Education for Critical Consciousness* (1973a) details his criticisms of the traditional education. *Pedagogy of
the Oppressed* (1970a) and *Cultural Action for Freedom*
(1970b) continue his criticism.

Freire's criticism of the schools is religiously inspired to the
extent that Freire wants education to promote the true humanization of man. For Freire the theological enterprise and
the educational enterprise have the same purpose—to promote the liberation of man. In an interview (Freire, 1970f),
he made explicit the connection he sees between education
and theology:

How must my attitude be, for example, before the Word
of God? I think that my attitude cannot be the attitude
of an empty being waiting to be filled by the Word of
God. I think also that in order to listen to it, it is necessary
to be engaged in the process of the liberation of man.
Because of this, I think that theology, such a theology,
should be connected with education for liberation—and

education for liberation with theology. (Freire, 1970f, p. 17.)

Since he has been with the World Council of Churches Freire's concerns have become increasingly theological. In this capacity, he addresses many religious groups. The religious dimension was present in earlier works but less explicit. As has been shown above, however, his fundamental view of man and reality is religious.

Freire's Criticism of Society. At first sight the influence of Freire's religious vision on his social philosophy and social criticism is not apparent. This philosophy appears to be both phenomenological and Marxist. Freire writes of the various levels of consciousness through which societies pass on their way to full development. He is Marxist in describing the conflict that exists between classes in society, and in proclaiming the necessity of a revolution to bring about the radical changes that must come in the societies of the underdeveloped world. *Pedagogy of the Oppressed* (1970a) and *Cultural Action for Freedom* (1970b) are replete with references to the writings of the neo-Marxists and other social analysts who are outside his religious tradition if not explicitly opposed to that tradition. In these writings, Freire utilizes such Marxist concepts as the class struggle, man's work as praxis, the necessity of political revolution, the function of ideology, and the inevitability of the dialectic or dialogue. Freire's use of these concepts will be explained later.

It is my contention that notwithstanding Freire's extensive use of nonreligious sources, his social philosophy is still consonant with a religious vision which he shares with many Christian thinkers, especially radical Christian thinkers in Latin America. In fact, a certain paradox may be found in the case of Freire. As he has become more Marxist, the religious inspiration of his social philosophy has become more explicit.

In *Education for Critical Consciousness* (1973a), Freire proposes a social philosophy of Christian democracy. This book recounts Freire's efforts to implement some of the reforms of the Goulart government through his literacy programs. Freire does not espouse Marxist views in this work. His analysis of Brazilian society describes the gradual awakening of consciousness through which Brazil was passing. The failure of governmental reforms was judged to be due to the Brazilian people's lack of experience with democracy. The goal of the Goulart administration, and of Freire who worked within it, was not revolution but the democratization of the culture. Freire details reasons for the failure of this democratic experience, drawing heavily on the work of Freyre (1964).

Freire's religious vision comes through in *La educación como práctica de la libertad* (1969) in a number of ways. He tells us that the fullness of man's existence is found in his union with his Creator, a union that safeguards man's freedom. Freire speaks of human existence as "a dynamic concept, implying eternal dialogue between man and man, between man and the world, between man and his Creator. It is this dialogue which makes of man an historical being" (Freire, 1969, p. 18). Freire describes his position toward social change as a radical Christian position which is indebted to the thought of Emmanuel Mounier, a twentieth-century French Christian philosopher. Freire, like other leftist Catholic intellectuals, drew heavily on the thought of Mounier, Teilhard de Chardin, the Jesuit scholar, and Jacques Maritain in order to bring the Christian emphasis on personal freedom, social activism, and change to bear on modern problems and movements. Freire (1973a) quotes at length from Mounier's article on Christianity and the concept of progress. Freire (1973a, p. 16) also quotes from Pope John XXIII's encyclical letter "Christianity and Social Progress" in establishing the proper kind of relationship that should exist among men and nations, a relationship of assistance without self-interest.

The democratic society that Freire proposes in *Education for Critical Consciousness* (1973a) is clearly to be founded on

Christian principles of freedom, justice, equality, and charity. References to Christian sources are not numerous, but they are significant. Man's awareness of and his living out of his relationship with his Creator is one of the important ingredients of the critical consciousness that is essential for the development of the new man and the new society (Freire, 1973a, pp. 17–18). The education that Freire proposes to help bring about this democratic society is described in religious terms borrowed from Karl Jaspers and Martin Buber, two other religious existentialists who have influenced his thinking. Educational dialogue for Freire is "nourished by love, humility, hope, faith, and trust. When the two 'poles' of the dialogue are thus linked by love, hope, and mutual trust, they can join in a critical search for something" (Freire, 1973a, p. 45).

The basic principles of a Christian social democratic philosophy are also found in *Pedagogy of the Oppressed* (1970a). Freire addressed his book to both Christians and Marxists, though he expected disagreement from both. He is sensitive to the point that revolutionaries may tend to dismiss him because of certain concepts in his writings. These concepts are those that obviously come from his religious vision: ontological vocation, love, dialogue, hope, humility, and sympathy (Freire, 1970a, p. 21). When Freire speaks of the necessity of violence or rebellion, these are always termed acts of love (1970a, pp. 41, 77). The fatalism of oppressed groups is attributed to a false concept of God (Freire, 1970a, p. 67). He rejects the concept that the oppressors are the defenders of Western civilization (1970a, p. 135). Some elements of the Marxist critique of society are introduced into *Pedagogy of the Oppressed* (1970a), and herein lies its advance over *Educação como prática da liberdade* (1967). Freire involves himself in analyzing the class struggles that exist in developing countries. Yet these Marxist elements are integrated with the principles that underlie the Christian view of society. Freire maintains his belief in God as controlling history through men. He also maintains his basically religious view of man.

Increasingly in later writings and speeches, he sees the Christian gospel as proclaiming the radical reordering of a society in which men are oppressed. He appeals not only to the gospel but also to social encyclicals of Popes John XXIII and Paul VI. At a talk in Rome in 1970 he made these comments:

> I am not yet completely a Catholic; I just keep on trying to be one more completely, day after day. . . . I just feel passionately, corporately, physically, with all my being, that my stance is a Christian one because it is 100 percent revolutionary and human and liberating, and hence committed and utopian. (Quoted in Donohue, 1972, p. 170.)

Freire's espousal of both the Christian and Marxist gospels is not surprising in light of developments within the Catholic left in Latin America starting with the late 1950's. This Catholic left, which had been nourished on the Christian humanism and Christian democracy of Mounier and Maritain, found itself working for social change more and more with members of the Communist Party and committed Marxists. Many in the Catholic left became increasingly interested in socialistic ideals. They attempted to maintain fundamental Christian beliefs while still incorporating socialist concepts that had previously been scorned by church authorities. The "Base Document" drawn up by the Catholic Popular Action group in 1962 at the Dominican convent in Belo Horizonte is a manifestation of this attempt (Sanders, 1967). From the social teaching of the church, this document posited a historical movement leading toward socialization and a concept of man as subject and end of the process. It also included an emphasis on economic conditioning, class struggle, imperialism, and the inevitable revolution. In language that finds many parallels in the writings of Freire, Popular Action "opted for a policy of revolutionary preparation, consisting of a mobilization of the people, on the basis of the development of their levels of consciousness and organization, securing this mobilization in a struggle against the double domination of capitalism (international and national) and feudalism" (Sanders, 1967, p. 600).

Freire's assimilation of Marxist ideas into a fundamental Christian vision finds many parallels in other Latin-American Christian thinkers (Colonnese, 1970, 1971; MacEoin, 1971; Quigley 1971). The various statements of the Latin-American bishops' conferences indicate a Marxist analysis of the social, economic, and political situations existing in Latin-American countries. These statements have shied away from proposing socialist revolution as the necessary solution to these problems. Individual bishops, such as Helder Camara of Recife, Brazil, and Sergeo-Mendes of Cuernavaca, Mexico, have proposed socialist solutions. Various groups of Christians, including priests, have advocated the necessity of a socialist revolution along the lines of Cuba (*First Encounter,* 1973, pp. 1–6).

Latin-American Christians who have attempted to forge a marriage of Christianity and Marxism have opened themselves to criticism from more orthodox members of both ideologies. Orthodox Christians contend that Marxism is essentially contradictory to fundamental Christian beliefs because of its espousal of materialism, determinism, and atheism. For these Christians, a person embraces Marxism only at the expense of abandoning his Christian faith. Many Marxists are equally convinced of the fundamental incompatibility of Marxism with religion. Even the efforts of humanistic or revisionist Marxists are rejected as contrary to orthodox Marxist doctrines. It is upon these revisionists or neo-Marxists, such as Althusser (1970) and Kolakowski (1968) that Freire depends, drawing much on the writings of the younger Marx.

Critique of Illich's and Freire's Social Criticism

My comparison of the social criticism of Paulo Freire and Ivan Illich has uncovered a number of similarities between these two men. Both men proceed in their social criticism from a religious view of man and society. They see present societies so constituted that they go counter to what is in the best interests of man as these interests are made clear in the religious tradition which they embrace. Both men have engaged in criticisms of the churches, schools and education, and other institutions of society. Both view the problems of education as central to society's problems.

One major difference was found to exist between the two men. Illich sees the church as an apolitical institution whose only political task is to urge its members to become involved in a critique of society. Freire, on the other hand, urges the churches to become involved in the task of changing society. This difference will be seen more clearly in the next chapter when I develop the theories of revolution that both men present.

Illich's societal criticism is impressive. I believe that Illich is correct in detailing many of the problems that have come with heavily industrialized societies. Where Illich fails, I believe, is in his attempts to give criteria for a new society. His proposals, and the philosophy underlying them, call for a return to the world as it was before industrialization, that is, to the medieval world. He identifies bigness, closeness, and sameness with goodness. I see no reason why the institutions that he proposes, if they were truly feasible and adequate to the needs of contemporary men, would not in time fall victim to the same sorts of criticisms that he levels against present institutions. Illich's social criticism may have a value as a utopian view by which concrete proposals for institutional growth could be evaluated. His criticism is based upon certain human values that are to be preserved. But other ways of preserving these are possible without returning to the medieval type of society that Illich proposes as postindustrial.

Freire's social criticism, while well-intentioned, can be termed vague, general, and imprecise. No adequate empirical basis for his criticism is presented. Freire is too prone to divide societies into good and bad without offering adequate criteria by which this division is made. Freire's analysis of Brazilian society appears inadequate when compared to other analyses made by social scientists. In his analysis of the role of the church in Latin America, Freire does not adequately indicate how the church which he proposes as part of the solution to the problem is really an essential part of the problem itself.

The social criticism of Freire and Illich has provided us with an introduction to the political thought of these two men. This political thought is seen foremost in the type of revolution each proposes to bring about the kind of society that he envisions.

4

Preachers of Revolution

Both Ivan Illich and Paulo Freire propose revolutions in their various writings. Freire's *Pedagogy of the Oppressed* (1970a) has been called "a handbook for revolutionary education" (Weaver, 1972, p. 1). The revolution he proposes is both political and cultural, intended to bring about a radical restructuring of society. Although Freire's emphasis is on political revolution, he sees a liberating education as a necessary condition for bringing about the revolution. *Pedagogy of the Oppressed* describes the type of education that must take place in order to initiate a revolution among oppressed people.

Illich also proclaims a revolution. His interest, however, is not in political revolutions, for he asserts that experience has proved that these revolutions leave the essential social problems of the countries unsolved. He points to the failure of socialist revolutions in both Russia and Cuba to bring about authentic freedom and "socialist" justice for the peoples of these countries (Illich, 1970, p. 46). In various places in his writings, he reserves judgment about the current revolution in China. The revolution that Illich proposes is a "cultural revolution":

> We need an alternative program, an alternative both to development and to merely political revolution. Let me call this alternative program either institutional or cul-

tural revolution, because its aim is the transformation of both public and personal reality. (Illich, 1969, p. 180.)

Illich (1970, 1973b, 1974, 1975) gives additional details on this cultural revolution.

Illich and Freire both see education as an essential element in their revolutionary program. Both men relate their revolutionary theories to their religious beliefs, but there are notable differences between them. Again the particular religious beliefs of both men are useful tools for understanding and comparing their visions of revolution. We will also look at other aspects of their thought on revolution.

Religious Dimension of Freire's Theory of Revolution

Freire has the reputation of an educator who proposes education as a necessary means for achieving revolution. *Pedagogy of the Oppressed* is virtually a handbook outlining the type of education that is necessary for bringing about drastic political and social changes in society. What is not so clearly recognized is that Freire has never participated in the type of revolutionary activity that he propounds in this book. He makes this clear in the preface:

It is possible that some may question my right to discuss revolutionary action, a subject of which I have no concrete experience. However, the fact that I have not personally participated in revolutionary action does not negate the possibility of my reflecting on this theme. (Freire, 1970a, p. 24.)

Freire contends that in his experience as an educator, he has "accumulated a comparative wealth of material which challenged [him] to run the risk of making the affirmations contained in this work" (1970a, p. 24).

Weffort (1969) in his introduction to *Educação como prática da liberdade* clearly explains the sense in which Freire's work in Brazil may be considered revolutionary. Freire's goals were literacy for the Brazilian masses and increased popular political participation. Freire was engaged in attempts to democratize Brazilian culture as a member of the Federal Ministry of Education. His work was viewed as revolutionary by certain rightist groups. Weffort described how Freire's work might be considered revolutionary:

> If education for freedom [Freire's literacy campaign] carried the seed of revolt, it would not be correct to say that this is one of the educator's objectives. If it occurs, it is only and exclusively because conscientization discerns a reality in which violence and conflict are the most frequent data. (Weffort, 1969, p. 11.)

Weffort criticizes the Popular Culture Movement, of which Freire was a part, for its failure to be more political. He contends that the "forces interested in popular mobilization failed to perceive and exploit the implications that conscientization had for action" (1969, p. 11). He admits that the popular movements had political relevance. Their inability, however, to be truly effective politically resulted from the fact that these movements were "committed directly or indirectly to the government and thus to the existing institutions which were themselves the objects of popular pressure" (Weffort, 1969, p. 9). The Popular Culture Movement failed because of an overinvestment in education at the expense of concrete political goals and strategies. Weffort (1969, p. 29) suggests that reformers like Freire were prevented from bringing about necessary changes for the masses because of the state support they received. They were in this way compromised by conflicting loyalties.

A reading of *Educação como prática da liberdade* (1967), a work written immediately after Freire's exile from Brazil and begun while he was in jail, shows no evidence of a revolutionary thrust. While working in Brazil he desired only to bring about changes gradually through education. The purpose of this education was to make the people aware of themselves as reflective human beings who created both history and culture. His literacy campaign was promoted by the Goulart government for at least one political purpose—the enfranchisement of the masses, who would then support the government in the upcoming elections.

In *Pedagogy of the Oppressed* Freire explicitly turned his attention to education as a necessary means for bringing about a revolution. Reasons for this conversion have been given earlier in this book. As I have already indicated, *Pedagogy of the Oppressed* is not based on experience in revolutionary movements. This explains some of the disillusionment that one encounters in reading Freire or in attending training sessions at which he appears. People expect an active revolutionary, but they meet "another religious, middle-class reformer" (Egerton, 1973, p. 34). Egerton, at a conference in South Carolina, sums up the criticism of Freire:

> Freire is no more radical than most of us. There is no originality in what he says—it's the same old rap. He has lectured us, criticized our narrow focus on small problems, but his alternative—the global perspective—is stale rhetoric. He is a political and ideological theoretician, not an educator. There is nothing concrete and specific in what he says. (Egerton, 1973, p. 35.)

Freire, the revolutionary educator, advised public school teachers to work within the system to do the little that they can do there. He also advised them to do the great many things they can do outside this system. At a conference I attended at Fordham University in January 1972, similar criticisms of Freire were voiced.

Freire (1970a, 1972a, 1972b) has advocated political revolutions for countries in the Third World. In doing this, he has been sensitive to the question of whether or not political revolution, especially violent revolution, is justified according to Christian principles. The religious inspiration of revolutions has been discussed by a number of scholars (Arendt, 1963, pp. 18–20; Brinton, 1965, pp. 170–172). This question has long been discussed, especially in Catholic leftist circles in Latin America. It is an issue that has brought radical Catholics into conflict with church hierarchies in Latin-American countries. Houtart and Rousseau (1971) divided Latin-American Christians into four main categories with regard to their attitudes toward revolution in society. One group sees no need for changes in the existing social and political systems. A second group sees the need for some change but does not think that the church as an institution should be involved in directly working for these changes. A third group sees change as necessary and believes that the church should directly participate in this process. Houtart and Rousseau (1971) contend that this is the attitude of many laymen engaged in politics, and that it appears to be the attitude of the Catholic bishops conference held at Medellin in 1968. Finally, there is a fourth category of Latin-American Christians who believe that only violent revolution can effectively change the situation. These Christians commit themselves to the revolutionary process and collaborate with various Marxist movements. In recent years, as Houtart and Rousseau point out, a number of clergymen and theologians have joined the ranks of this latter group.

By 1970 Freire definitely put himself into league with this latter group of Christians. In speaking of the myths which the oppressor society has imposed upon the oppressed, he points to two in particular that bear on this issue: "The myth of the heroism of the oppressor classes as defenders of 'Western Christian civilization' . . . the myth that rebellion is a sin against God" (Freire, 1970a, pp. 135–136). The implication here, which is supported by more recent writings, is that Freire sees rebellion and revolution as acts that can be in accord with Christian and religious principles. Freire describes revolutionary violence in terms that have at least religious connotations:

> I am more and more convinced that true revolutionaries must perceive the revolution, because of its creative and

liberating nature, as an act of love. For me, the revolution which is not possible without a theory of revolution —and therefore science—is not irreconcilable with love. (Freire, 1970a, p. 77.)

Recent writings show Freire even more explicit in his justification of Christian participation in revolutionary action. In the "Letter to a Theology Student" (Freire, 1972b), he asserted:

We, as Christians, have an enormous task to perform, presuming that we are capable of setting aside our idealistic myths and in that way sharing in the revolutionary transformation of society, instead of stubbornly denying the important contribution of Karl Marx. (Freire, 1972b, p. 7.)

He affirms in the letter that the Word of God demands a willingness to work for the liberation of man through a process that entails the challenging of the powerful of the earth (Freire, 1972b, p. 7).

Freire's most explicit treatment of the religious justification for revolutionary action is found in his article "The Educational Role of the Churches in Latin America" (Freire, 1972a). He repeated these ideas in "Education, Liberation, and the Church" (Freire, 1973b). The church, he contended, cannot remain neutral toward political activity (Freire, 1972a, p. 1). It must work for the radical transformation of social structures. He criticized conservatives in the churches for "castrating the church's prophetic dimension and fearing the radical transformation of the unjust world" (Freire, 1972a, p. 3). He had praise for the developing political theology of liberation which says something about the revolutionary transformation of the world. Within this prophetic theology there is room for the view that recognizes "revolution as the road to liberation for the oppressed classes, and the military coup as a revolutionary option" (Freire, 1972a, p. 12). He admits that there may be differences over tactics among Christians dedicated to revolutionary action, but he commends the firm commitment of these Christians to revolutionary action (Freire, 1972a, p. 12).

Two religious metaphors are used by Freire in urging Christians to become involved in revolutionary activity. He refers a number of times to the revolution of the oppressed as a Passover or an Easter. These events entailed struggles of life and death. Redemption or liberation from oppression was achieved through active resistance and violent death. Thus Christians who participate in revolutionary action against oppression, as we saw in Chapter 3, take part in a new Passover, a new Easter. The revolutionaries' "setting out is really a sort of Passover in which they will have to die as an oppressed class, in order to be reborn as a class that liberates itself" (Freire, 1972a, p. 4). He speaks of the prophetic church which does not allow itself to be made a refuge for the oppressed masses, but rather invites them to a new exodus (Freire, 1972a, p. 12).

Another encouragement that Freire utilizes in urging Latin-American Christians into revolutionary activity lies in the example of the Christ. The image of Christ is that of a radical, not satisfied with the *status quo,* anxious to move on, willing to die in order to bring about a continuous rebirth (Freire, 1972a, p. 11). Freire puts these words in the mouth of those who would counsel conservative activity on the part of Christians: "They say to Christ, 'Master, why push on, if everything here is so beautiful?' " (Freire, 1972a, p. 12).

An interesting development can be discerned in the writings of Freire. He has become an advocate of revolutionary action for oppressed peoples in the Third World. The difference between *Educação como prática da liberdade* (1967) and *Pedagogy of the Oppressed* (1970a) makes this clear. This change, however, has been accompanied by a change from a less explicit religious justification of revolution to a more explicit necessity for Christian participation in revolutionary activity. The failure to become involved in this type of action in certain countries in Latin America is a failure "to live up to the Gospel" (Freire, 1972a, p. 5). (It will be shown that on this point the gospel according to Freire differs greatly from the gospel according to Illich.)

Freire's open advocacy of revolution on religious principles finds much support among Latin-American theologians with whom Freire is familiar. He has expressed a desire to meet with Latin-American theologians who propose a political theology of liberation (Freire, 1970f, p. 17). Freire's position on the religious justification for revolution is similar to that of Gustavo Gutiérrez, one of Latin America's leading Christian theologians. Gutierrez has attempted to give religious justification for the more revolutionary political postures of Christian groups in Latin America. He appeals to the message of the gospel:

> What ultimately brings Christians to participate in liberating oppressed peoples is the conviction that the gospel message is radically incompatible with an unjust society. They see clearly that they cannot be authentic christians unless they act. (Gutiérrez, 1971, p. 72.)

Gutiérrez discusses revolution in the context of the Biblical symbols of creation, salvation, and the prophetic promises for a kingdom of peace. The case for active church involvement in revolution is put strongly in these terms:

> In Latin America, the church must realize that it exists in a continent undergoing revolution, where violence is present in different ways. The world in which the Christian community is called on to live . . . is one in social revolution. Its mission must be achieved keeping that in account. The church has no alternative. Only a total break with the unjust order to which it is bound in a thousand conscious or unconscious ways, and a forthright commitment to a new society, will make men in Latin America believe the message of love it bears. (Gutiérrez, 1971, pp. 76–77.)

Freire, on a number of occasions in his writings, makes reference to the example of Camilo Torres, the Colombian priest-sociologist who became involved in politics and was ultimately killed as a guerrilla. Freire admired the commitment of Torres to the people—as a priest, as a Christian, and as a revolutionary (Freire, 1970a, p. 162). Torres is referred to as the guerrilla priest, a loving man (Freire, 1970a, p. 171; 1970b, p. 45). Torres made a serious attempt to articulate a theory of liberation consonant with orthodox Christian values (Goulet, 1971; Petras, 1968). Torres stated that the Catholics in Colombia had a moral responsibility to participate in the revolution (Celestin, 1969). A current study attempts to connect the thought of Torres, Freire, and other theologians of liberation (Grabowski, 1972, p. 132).

Religious Dimension of Illich's Theory of Revolution

Illich, like Freire, proposes a revolution for society, both for developed and developing countries. But unlike Freire, he puts little emphasis on a political revolution. He terms his alternative program either institutional or cultural revolution. Illich first described this alternative in his essay "A Constitution for Cultural Revolution" (Illich, 1969, pp. 175–189). Political revolution is inadequate for Illich because it fails to strike at the heart of modern ills—the very nature of the institutions that man has fashioned. These institutions form the consciousness of modern man; they offer their products as the only true human values and produce needless demands. Education, in this essay, is the paramount example of a manipulative modern institution. The true cultural revolutionary in this area would work to abolish compulsory schooling and discriminatory tests for hiring. He would also attempt to have an equal amount of money allocated for the education of each person in society. Finally, the cultural revolutionary in the area of education would work to break up the monopoly that the schools have over education.

In *Deschooling Society* (1970), Illich describes the revolutionary potential of deschooling. He argues against the neo-

Marxist analysts who "say that the process of deschooling must be postponed or bracketed until other disorders, traditionally understood as more fundamental, are corrected by an economic and political revolution" (Illich, 1970, p. 46). Illich uses deschooling as the measure to evaluate all revolutionary political programs. For him, a political revolution without deschooling necessarily fails to attack the basic ills of society, which are centered around the alienated patterns of consumption. The school, more than any other institution, reproduces this consumer society. This happens in all countries "be they fascist, democratic, or socialist, big or small, rich or poor" (Illich, 1970, p. 74).

Illich gives a somewhat clearer exposition of the institutional revolution he proposes in his work *Tools for Conviviality* (1973b). He sees the imminent breakdown of industrial society (p. 102). Men must begin to recognize the natural limits that must be placed on all human endeavors. This revolution will be a peaceful one. It will be accomplished by a voting majority, not by a party or a sect (Illich, 1973b, p. 108). The revolution is to be achieved through legal procedures. Majorities that will work for the new society will develop out of enlightened self-interest. With the eruption of smoldering conflicts into political actions, "new elites" will arise to "provide an interpretative framework for new—and hitherto unexpected—alignments of interest" (Illich, 1973b, p. 102).

The society of the future that Illich proposes is a frugal society. This society will result from a political choice by the people. He asserts:

> The alternative to managerial fascism is a political process by which people decide how much of any scarce resource is the most any member can claim; a process in which they agree to keep limits relatively stationary over a long time, and by which they set a premium on

the constant search for new ways to have an ever larger
percentage of the population join in doing ever more
with ever less. (Illich, 1973b, p. 101.)

Illich readily admits the enormity of the task. "With the
possible exception of China under Mao, no present government could restructure society along convivial lines" (Illich,
1973b, p. 16). Consequently, Illich does not deal in this work
with political strategies or tactics. He restricts himself to a
description of basic structural criteria within which the cultural revolution can take place. (Actually, Illich does present
what he considers to be political and legal tools for establishing and protecting the convivial society [Illich, 1973b, pp.
99ff.].) The distinction between "tactics and strategies" on
the one hand and "political and legal tools" on the other is
not made clear.

Illich's revolution, like Freire's, has a religious quality to it.
The religious vision is not made explicit in *Tools for Conviviality,* but nonetheless it appears at crucial parts of Illich's
argument. The religious dimension of Illich's cultural revolution, however, comes out more explicitly in talks before religious groups. Though it could be contended that he merely
adds the religious dimension on these occasions to accommo-
date himself to his audience, I believe that the opposite is the
case. The religious inspiration of his thought is fundamental,
although it appears only implicitly in works addressed to
general audiences. This assertion can be justified by an excur-
sion into the nature of Illich's theological method.

Illich's theological method which underpins all his thinking has led some of his critics to misunderstand him. Gintis
(1972) sees Illich as employing merely the method of total
criticism and negation. "Illich's failures can be consistently
traced to his refusal to pass *beyond* negations—beyond a
total rejection of the appearances of life in advanced industrial societies—to a higher synthesis." (Gintis, 1972, p. 94.)
Illich utilizes the apophatic logic of classical negative theology to construct his arguments. (Apophatic logic makes asser-

tions through denials.) One sees this method in the little-known collections of essays by and on Illich (Eychaner, 1970). In these essays, Illich constructs a theology in which silence is man's highest form of communication; poverty is the means for carrying out human acts that are most meaningful, creative, and rich; powerlessness is the most effective tool for demonstrating authoritative control. Illich develops a theological view in which the autonomy of the spontaneous and surprising in human life is valued more than the planned, in which the ludicrous is preferred to the useful, and the gratuitous accepted more readily than the purposeful (Eychaner, 1970, pp. 8–9).

In the essays in which these ideas are developed, Illich is addressing future missioners in Latin America. The chief virtue that the future missioner will need is Christian renunciation. He must renounce worldly goods and possessions (Eychaner, 1970, pp. 110–111). His life must be one of sacrifice and poverty. The missioner must be willing to renounce some of his freedom in order that he might advance the freedom and maturity of others. The missioner is to be a living witness to values that go counter to the values present in existing cultures.

In negative theology, the truth is arrived at by pursuing the opposite of that to which human reasoning leads. It is the method of Augustine of Hippo and of many Christian mystics. Illich's convivial society sounds quite similar to Augustine's City of God. It is the opposite of present existing societies. It is constructed by denying the evil qualities of the city of man. Acceptance of this society takes the person to the boundaries of faith. Gintis may want Illich to go beyond negations to the development of synthesis, but such a suggestion is unacceptable to any true mystic.

The religious impulse in Illich's revolutionary program comes through in *Tools for Conviviality* in a number of interesting ways. In explaining the meaning of "convivial," he appeals to Thomas Aquinas' treatment of the virtue of *eutrapelia*. Illich explains this virtue as austerity, and he sees it as including only those enjoyments which do not distract from or destroy personal relatedness. Illich's call to cultural revolution is a call to a religious-like austerity in which one is keenly aware that things or tools can destroy rather than enhance personal relationships (Illich, 1973b, p. xxv).

Renunciation is a predominant theme in convivial reconstruction. Illich (1973b) argues that "survival in justice is possible only at the cost of those sacrifices implicit in the adoption of a convivial mode of production and the universal renunciation of unlimited progeny, affluence, and power on the part of both individuals and groups" (1973b, p. xxv). Illich maintains that people need to rediscover the value of joyful sobriety and liberating austerity. A joyful renunciation—voluntary poverty, self-control, abstinence from unlimited consumption and use—is part of his "religious" revolutionary program (Illich, 1973b, p. 65). Like the prophets declaring the imminent destruction of Jerusalem or Jesus proclaiming the end time of human existence, Illich proclaims the coming crisis, the breakdown of industrial society (1973b, p. 102). He gives the reasons for the coming crisis. He foresees a possible unexpected event like the Great Depression that will trigger the crisis. "We still have a chance to understand the causes of the coming crisis, and to prepare for it" (Illich, 1973b, p. 104). His book is a description of these causes and presents plans for action in the face of the coming disaster. A voting majority in each country can use legal means to accomplish social reconstruction.

Illich (1972c) makes the religious nature of his revolutionary program most explicit in his article "How Can We Hand On Christianity?" In this article he calls for the convergence of two movements: "social criticism, which is truly radical, and Christian prophesy, which is independent and free" (Illich, 1972c, p. 18). Illich urges the radicals in politics to make the Sermon on the Mount the principal theme in their programs. The gospel today demands the voluntary imposition of limits to certain technological dimensions. The gospel demands that community limits should be set as to what shall be enough and therefore good enough for each society (Illich, 1973b, p. 19).

Participation in the cultural revolution appears to have all the signs of a religious crusade for Illich. Speaking to a group in Lima, Peru, in 1971, Illich (1972b), the prophet for cultural revolution and the convivial society, spoke in these terms:

> In the name of God, we must denounce the idolatry of progress and the polluting escalation of production. . . . We must remind men that God has created a good world and [we must] cherish it without the need of an intermediary. . . . Consequently, we must refuse to cooperate in any attempt to create a man-made environment in which the lives of all persons would depend on their having been clients of a service organization. (Illich, 1972b, p. 47.)

Illich details the courage that will be needed to participate in this revolution. It will entail the structuring of a world in which radical limits are agreed to by a majority. Illich sees this antitechnocratic consensus as easily translatable into the poverty, powerlessness, and nonviolence of the Christian gospel. He affirms his belief that the most rational policy for this world in which there is an ever-increasing gap between the rich and the poor is this Christian message of self-chosen poverty, powerlessness, and nonviolence (Illich, 1972b, p. 48).

With regard to the religious dimension of their revolutionary impulses, there are significant differences between Illich and Freire. Freire, as has been shown, urges the church to become involved in political and social movements for liberation. In his recent essay "The Educational Role of the Churches in Latin America" (1972a), Freire argues that the churches must turn toward political activity. These churches must identify with the oppressed peoples of the Third World. Illich, on the other hand, does not want to see church involvement in direct political action. Illich maintains that there must be a clear distinction between the mission of the church and any particular social or political program. The church will jeopardize its true nature and mission if it becomes involved in particular political and social programs (Eychaner, 1970, pp. 17ff.). In another writing on this subject, Illich (1972c) speaks of the church as a place of peace and repose where people may be connected with past traditions and enjoy an aspect of life that is separated from the changes taking place in society.

The mystical strain exists in Illich's personality. There is also present the true believer in the religious dimension of life and in the church as a purely spiritual organization. What the world needs, according to Illich, is a revolution in which this deeply religious spirit permeates the men who control and set limits to the institutions of society. Illich (1972c) tells us what his preferred life-style is for the 1970's:

> I would like to work with a group of people at filling out a matrix listing in one direction certain forms of behavior which in the old way I would identify as explicitly formal prayer forms, such as silence, or waking at night, or abstention or good gourmet eating on certain occasions, feasting or even orgiastic behavior or common recitation of poems. (Illich, 1972c, p. 18.)

Illich would draw on various mystic traditions: Sufistic, Jewish, Christian. The aims of the group Illich would like to work with would be to search for the presence of God and to find the basic form of religious community. Another aim would be "to see if we could not seek the visibility of the church in the conscious, evangelical interpretation of prayer rather than in the evangelical interpretation of some political or organizational structure" (Illich, 1972c, p. 18). People guided by the principles of the Christian gospel should join in the world of social and political change. But the Christian community as such "must become the place, the moment, the space which we, by common agreement, reserve in this passing, changing world, for the commemoration of the Lord— a place, a space, for seeing, as much as we can, how we extend the tradition in which this commemoration is performed" (Illich, 1972c, p. 18).

Freire's views on this pattern of church participation in revolutionary change is much more acceptable to Latin Americans who are working for change. There is little possibility for the church to diminish its social and political roles in these countries in the near future. There is also little hope that it will deinstitutionalize itself along the lines that Illich desires. In the light of these realities, those Christians like Freire and liberal clergy and laity are correct in their efforts to press for church support in effecting needed changes in Latin America. Illich may propose a revolution in which the message of the gospel on poverty, nonviolence, and powerlessness will change the face of the earth. The catastrophe that Illich predicts may or may not be imminent. But his solution, which fails to take with full seriousness the overriding issue of power, appears rather simplistic. No one can seriously expect the church to disengage itself from social and political struggles in any country. The clear distinction that Illich attempts to draw between the mission of the church and the task of secular society does not come off.

Illich contends that the gospel has been misused by both sides in controversies over social, political, and economic issues. From this he argues, in order not to contaminate itself, the church should not become involved in these types of controversies. He betrays here his own theological conservatism. The Scriptures do not present one view on each disputed matter. They portray the attempts of religious communities to come to grips with all the various problems they have faced. Differences of opinion exist within the original writings themselves. Consequently, one is not to be surprised if people have utilized these writings in arriving at different conclusions at different times.

Both Illich and Freire are rather selective in their use of the Christian tradition. Both cloak their particular interpretation of this tradition with the mantle of "the gospel." This is true of many other groupings of Christians. Some look to the Scriptures for justification of pacifism; others, for a "just war" theory or for agonized participation in warfare. What this indicates about Freire and Illich is that they have arrived at different conclusions on this matter because of differing interpretations of their religious tradition.

Freire's Theory and Strategy of Revolution

It has already been mentioned that Freire has had no direct involvement with revolutionary activity. He indicates that he has received insights into this activity from his educational experiences in Brazil and Chile. His theory of revolution developed in a most eclectic manner. He draws on the writings of Mao Tse-tung, Marcuse, Fanon, Debray, Che Guevara, Marx, Lenin, Castro, and others. Illich's revolutionary program, on the other hand, does not draw on these classical revolutionary theorists. His cultural revolution is to be achieved through a process of "political inversion" and the recovery of legal procedure. Illich has been influenced in his thinking in this area by a group of radical lawyers who met at Cuernavaca in the early 1970's (Weisstub, 1972).

Freire's theory and strategy of revolution appear to be rather naïve, to use a favorite word of his in *Pedagogy of the Oppressed* (1970a). He discusses revolution without discussing any particular social and historical contexts. He appears to be generalizing from his reflections upon the Brazilian situations in which he was involved. He is like the crusader who, after the brave and good fight, stands ready to generalize his theories and strategies to the situation of all oppressed peoples. *Pedagogy of the Oppressed* was written by Freire to tell himself what he and his fellow reformists should have done to bring about real change in Brazil in the early 1960's. But the simplistic analysis of Brazilian society into oppressed and oppressors does not do justice even to that historical situation. Its application as a universal theory of social analysis is even more unacceptable.

A fundamental flaw in Freire's theory of revolution is his

inadequate treatment of "oppression." For Freire, "any situation in which A objectively exploits B or hinders his pursuit of self-affirmation as a responsible person is one of oppression" (Freire, 1970a, p. 40). He further tells us that an act is oppressive when "it interferes with man's ontological and historical vocation to be more fully human" (Freire, 1970a, pp. 40–41). For Freire, the goal of liberation from oppression is the humanization of man. Oppression is always an act of violence. It is to treat a person as if he were a thing (Freire, 1970a, p. 45).

For Freire, the problem of oppression is reduced to the problem of dehumanization, and he appears to carry within him some intuitive concept of what it means to be human. Without spelling out his criteria for self-affirmation or humanization of the person, his description of oppression becomes not only abstract but also dangerous. Unless one sets down objective criteria for exploitation, determining what is oppressive becomes the judgment of each individual and group. Freire would certainly not affirm this. He is convinced that through his pedagogy the oppressed with their leaders will come to intuit reality the way it is. Freire's doctrine of objective exploitation comes dangerously close to the concept of the objective enemy which Arendt (1958) criticized:

> The chief difference between the despotic and the totalitarian secret police lies in the difference between the "suspect" and the "objective enemy." The latter is defined by the policy of the government and not by his own desire to overthrow it. (Arendt, 1958, p. 423.)

Freire sees only one relationship in the Third World, the relationship of oppression and subjection. Boston (1972, p. 88) indicates a number of other relationships that exist in the Third World. Even in more advanced technological countries Freire thinks only in terms of oppressor-oppressed relationships. The oppressors in these societies are those who use technology to manipulate people and to produce a mass society. Freire does not condemn technology in itself, but rather

its harmful effects. The treatment that Freire gives to technology is not extensive. But when he does treat man and
technology, the same type of relationship is seen—dependence, subjection, oppression (Freire, 1970a, pp. 48–50).

The tendency of Freire to see only one type of relationship
among men makes it most difficult to apply his pedagogy.
The cultural, the social, the political, the religious are all seen
in the same light. It is easy for Freire to do this in *Pedagogy
of the Oppressed* because he fails to root his revolutionary
theory in any particular historical or cultural context. In attempting to forge a universal theory of revolutionary
pedagogy, he oversimplifies to a dangerous degree the concept of oppression and the pedagogical program. He appears
to be unaware in *Pedagogy of the Oppressed* that revolutions
differ according to differing social and economic situations.
Freire's failure to link his revolutionary theory to a particular
historical situation makes his theory abstract, and separates
him from such theorists of revolution as Johnson (1966) and
Arendt (1963), who consider these contexts essential in defining revolution. It also renders his theory of pedagogy almost
impossible to apply, as many groups have found who have
begun to work with his ideas.

Freire considers his emphasis on the "dialogical nature" of
revolutionary action to be his main contribution to a theory
of revolution. Freire believes that leaders should be in constant dialogue with the people at all points in the revolution.
In fact, he points to his experience in "dialogical" and prob-
lem-solving education as giving him the necessary experience to write a book on revolutionary action in which he has
never participated (Freire, 1970a, p. 24). *Pedagogy of the
Oppressed* was written to defend the eminently pedagogical
character of the revolution (Freire, p. 54).

> Critical and liberating dialogue, which presupposes ac-
> tion, must be carried on with the oppressed at whatever
> the stage of their struggle for liberation. The content of
> that dialogue can and should vary in accordance with

historical conditions and the level at which they can perceive reality. (Freire, 1970a, p. 52.)

Freire's commitment to the dialogical character of the revolution is a rather limited one. After he indicates the number of cases where dialogue among equals is to be suspended, there is little left to his theory about the dialogical nature of the revolution. Freire has great difficulty in making his hero, Guevara, an advocate of dialogical revolutionary action. He quotes the revolutionary leader's words:

> Mistrust: at the beginning, do not trust your own shadow, never trust friendly peasants, informers, guides, or contact men. Do not trust anything or anybody until a zone is completely liberated. (Freire, 1970a, p. 169.)

Guevara advocates communion with the people after liberation has been achieved. This, however, does not, as Freire would wish it to, make Guevara an advocate of dialogue with the people at every stage of the revolution. Freire commends the realism of the guerrilla leader and still attempts to make him an advocate of Freire's theory of dialogue. But this appears impossible. In commending Guevara's mistrust of the ambiguity of oppressed men and refusal to dialogue with them, Freire has denied the very essence of his theory of revolutionary action as fundamentally dialogical.

Freire compromises his dialogical theory of revolution in a number of other instances. He denies the revolutionaries' need to dialogue with the former oppressors (Freire, 1970a, p. 134). He agrees with Guevara's admonition to punish the deserter from the revolutionary group. This must be done to preserve the cohesion and the discipline of the group (Freire, 1970a, p. 170). Freire agrees with the guerrilla leader in his nontolerance of those who are not ready to accept the conclusion that revolution is essential. He speaks of the revolution as loving and creating life: "And in order to create life, it [the revolution] may be obliged to prevent some men from circumscribing life" (Freire, 1970a, p. 171).

In *Pedagogy of the Oppressed* Freire valiantly attempts to

make his theory of the dialogical character of the revolution hold up against the stated views of revolutionaries. The effort must be pronounced a failure. The forging of a revolution would seem to preclude any dialogue among equals to arrive at truth by permitting the free expression of ideas (Debray, 1967, pp. 56, 111). The educator inexperienced in revolutionary activity, has exaggerated the role that the free educational process is to play in forging a revolution.

Freire's exaggerated role of dialogical activity in forging the revolution stems from a more fundamental problem, his inadequate treatment of education through dialogue. Briefly, it is Freire's position that somehow through dialogue people will come to see objective reality. In this process, they will denounce what is truly oppressive and at the same time announce or proclaim a new nonoppressive reality. In announcing this new reality, they are already engaged in the process of working for its concrete realization. Freire is convinced that total freedom must be ensured to people involved in such dialogue. It is Freire's philosophical position that an objective reality exists, which all will come to recognize through education. This fails to do justice to the complex nature of reality and of man's knowledge of it. It leaves little room for relativism and a pluralism of world views.

Freire is rather vague in his description of the process and strategy of revolution, as many writers on revolutionary theory, are. Revolutionary leadership will usually be made up of "men who in one way or another have belonged to the social strata of the dominators" (Freire, 1970a, p. 162). Inauthentic leaders will be made manifest through the practice of the dialectic. These leaders are to organize themselves with the people. Freire admits that he has no details on how the revolution is to take place:

> Instead of following predetermined plans, leaders and people, mutually identified, together create the guidelines of their action. In this synthesis, leaders and people

are somehow reborn in new knowledge and new action.
(Freire, 1970a, p. 183.)

Illich's Theory and Strategy of Revolution

While Freire proposes a revolution that is involved in the
violent take-over of power by an organized group of guerril-
las who are in communion with the people, Illich's cultural
revolution is in some ways a peaceful one. Illich predicts a
violent breakdown of the industrial system, similar to the
Great Depression. The institutions of society will lose their
respectability, and confidence will no longer be placed in the
managers of these institutions. He describes the possibilities:

> The inevitable catastrophic event could be either a crisis
> in civilization or its end: end by annihilation or end in
> B. F. Skinner's world-wide concentration camp run by a
> T. E. Frazier. The foreseeable catastrophe will be a true
> crisis—that is, the occasion for a choice—only if at the
> moment it strikes, the necessary social demands can be
> effectively expressed. (Illich, 1973b, pp. 105–106.)

Illich expects the managers of society's institutions to turn
to "new elites which can provide an interpretive framework
for new—and hitherto unexpected—alignments of interest"
(Illich, 1973b, p. 102). The group that will take over society
is defined was a voting majority. It is not a class of society like
the working class or a political party. It is rather a group of
people drawn from all parts of society. They will be united
only by their recognition of the depth of the industrial crisis
and by their acceptance of the necessity to place limits on
industrial growth (Illich, 1973b, p. 108.)

The means Illich proposes for achieving the cultural revolution is the efficacy of law and the potential of the democratic process. This assertion clearly removes Illich from his
anarchist admirers, for the true anarchist denies the validity
and usefulness of law (Shatz, 1971, p. xv). Illich places his

hope not in a body of laws or policies, but in the formal political process (Illich, 1973b, p. 94). He selects two complementary features of the formal structure: the inherent continuity of the system and the adversary procedure. The former feature ensures not only that new legislation has to be adapted to preceding legislation but also that new legislation is possible that would set limits to future growth. The adversary procedure provides a process by which citizens can take action against corporations even if these are agencies of the state.

Illich is quick to admit the weakness of the present legal systems for bringing about the type of revolution he proposes. Laws are used to manipulate people and keep them under the control of institutions. He also admits that the laws are often corrupted by industrial interests that go contrary to the interests of the people. He realizes that he might receive scorn from his fellow revolutionaries on this point. Yet he contends that the law is the only alternative to inevitable violence. He strongly asserts that "any revolution which neglects the use of formal, legal, and political procedures will fail. Only an active majority in which all individuals and groups insist for their own reasons on their own rights, and whose members share the same convivial procedure, can recover the rights of men against corporations" (Illich, 1973b, p. 99). Illich ends *Tools for Conviviality* with an act of faith in the formal structure of the law which is embedded in the history of mankind. For him it "remains the most powerful instrument to say the truth and denounce the cancerous domination of the industrial dominance over production as the ultimate form of idolatry" (Illich, 1973b, p. 110).

Illich's faith in the formal structure of law would not appear to be well founded. His presentation of law appears as a panacea, an instrument that can be used easily and effectively to achieve desired results. There is not much evidence that law is able to achieve major social changes. Law seems better suited to solidify changes that have already taken place. Deep-seated tensions in society that Illich speaks of involve groups with great self-interests. One needs only to think of the feeble efforts that were made through political procedures in recent years to end United States involvement in Indochina. According to Sousa Santos (1972, 17/17), Illich must project a catastrophe of even greater proportions than this to guarantee the efficacy of legal processes to address problems that involve deep-seated differences among groups in society.

Illich's faith in law and sense of justice among mankind come in part from his dependence on John Rawls's *A Theory of Justice* (1971). Illich does not quote Rawls in *Tools for Conviviality* (1973b), but he has indicated that Rawls's work was the single most important written contribution to the Seminar on Limits during July/August 1972 in Cuernavaca (Illich, 1972d, pp. 37/32). Illich's description of the just society closely resembles Rawls's principle of fairness:

> A just society would be one in which liberty for one person is constrained only by the demands created by equal liberty for another. Such a society requires as a precondition an agreement excluding tools that by their very nature prevent such liberty. (Illich, 1973b, p. 4.)

Illich appears to accept Rawls's principle of difference in admitting inequalities in his convivial society only in the case that tools are more widely distributed (Illich, 1973b, p. 17). The revolution will be accomplished because the sense of justice in people can be trusted to make the correct decisions in the time of industrial crisis. Those who have insight into the nature of the crisis will be able to convince their peers of the just and fair measures that ought to be taken to bring about and to maintain the convivial society.

One difference between Illich and Rawls is a point that Illich has come to through prodding of his socialist friends. Illich has shown a reluctance to identify himself as a socialist. But he clearly does so in *Tools for Conviviality* (Illich, 1973b, p. 15). Rawls sees the just society as neutral with regard to public or private ownership of the means of production. Illich accepts the necessity for "public ownership of resources and of the means of production, and public control over the market and over net transfers of powers" (Illich, 1973b, p. 43). But what is more important for Illich is that this public control and ownership must be complemented by "a public determination of the tolerable basic structure of modern tools" (Illich, 1973b, p. 43).

Apocalyptic and utopian thought thus converge in the new politics of Ivan Illich. Illich (1973b, p. 1) admits that his work is only a progress report and that he does not intend to "describe in detail any functional community of the future" (p. 14). He desires to provide guidelines for action but not political strategies and tactics (Illich, 1973b, p. 16). He has presented a fascinating discussion of law and political procedure. But he has given only the most vague directions for his new politics. His ideas can easily be assimilated into what environmental lawyers are presently doing to bring about changes. He fails to consider seriously the conflicting interest groups in society. He presents no analysis of what particular groups would make up his new voting majority. He never addresses himself to what form of government his convivial society would have or how it would relate to the new groups that would make up the majority.

A question keeps going through one's mind in reading *Tools for Conviviality.* Has Illich exaggerated the crisis in industrial society? It is not within the limits of this book to evaluate this question. Suffice it to say that a serious answer has been made to apocalyptic environmentalists such as Illich by Maddox (1972) and Neuhaus (1971). Illich's new politics appear to be developed in anticipation of the coming crisis. Perhaps warnings such as Illich's and the suggestions he presents concerning political processes will be instrumental in averting the type of crisis he presents as inevitable.

In this chapter Illich and Freire have been presented as the preachers of revolutions for society. Freire's ideas are concerned more with the Third World than with advanced industrial countries. He is thus concerned more with purely political revolutions. Illich is primarily concerned with the revolution that will take place in advanced industrial countries such as the United States. But he has the Third World in mind when he notes on the last page of *Tools for Conviviality* (1973b):

> Reconstruction for poor countries means adopting a set of negative design criteria within which their tools are kept, in order to advance directly into a post-industrial era of conviviality. The limits to choose are of the same order as those which hyper-industrialized countries will have to adopt for the sake of survival and at the cost of their vested interests. (Illich, 1973b, p. 110.)

The revolution that both men present is to be made in the name of man and in the name of God. For both of these men a primary focus of the revolutionary must be upon education and schooling. The remaining chapters will be concerned with the role of education and schooling in helping to forge political or cultural revolutions.

5

Radical Critics
of Education

Ivan Illich is considered by many to be one of the most radical critics of schooling. Paulo Freire is regarded as the originator of a revolutionary pedagogy which is adaptable to the oppressed in all countries of the world. His criticisms of the schools and of education, though not quite so extensive as that of Illich, are increasingly cited by educators in various parts of the world. In this chapter, the critique to which both of these men subject schooling will be compared, contrasted, and evaluated.

Religious Vision and Educational Criticism

One of the major themes of this book has been to show how the particular religious visions of Illich and Freire have influenced their thought in various areas. This religious dimension has also been a useful instrument for comparing and evaluating their thought. I have already mentioned in passing how their religious visions influence their educational criticism. Let us now be more explicit.

Ivan Illich. While Illich was still deeply involved in a critique of the institutional church, he began to turn his attention to the problems of educational systems, especially in developing countries. Through his association with Everett Reimer, first in Puerto Rico and then in Mexico, he began to see parallels between the problems of the church and those

98

of the schools. Illich draws many analogies in his writings on the schools to problems that exist in the church and have parallels in schools and other institutions. What is not generally recognized is that Illich first turned to an analysis of the schools to find parallels for what was happening in the church. Illich (1972c) states:

> One of my reasons for studying and writing about educational matters was to provide an analysis, a comparison for what has happened to the church: to see the peculiar form, the degraded form of a world-wide obligatory school system which the church has become. (1972c, p. 21.)

Illich has come to see in the schools and in other institutions of society the same destructive tendencies that he saw in the church. All these institutions turn values into commodities. Illich contends that true religion and faith cannot take place in a service institution which imitates the industrial mode of production. His vision of the church is a place where, he states:

> We can provide the things, the events, the people to which somebody called by the Lord needs access if he wants to approach Christ, leaving it up to the Lord to show those who come after us how these things happened in our generation. (Illich, 1972c, p. 21.)

Illich's church is to provide an atmosphere of freedom where people may congregate to celebrate the religious tradition in which they were reared (Illich, 1972c, p. 21).

All the ills that Illich sees in the schools and in other institutions of society he first of all saw in the institution of the Catholic Church, of which he is still a member. His attack on these institutions is based on his views on man, community, and the institution which have been derived from the Christian humanistic tradition in which he is situated. Many have pointed to the theological analogies and metaphors in his writings, but the peculiar type of theological criticism has not been sufficiently investigated. The entire corpus of Illich's writings must be examined to see the fundamental religious character of his work.

Illich's fundamental criticism of the church is that its excessive institutionalization has defeated the original purpose for which it was established. According to Illich the church has passed its "second watershed" (Illich, 1973b, p. 1). This point is reached when the harmful side effects of the institutionalization of a value, such as religion, education, transportation, social service, serve to cancel out the fundamental purposes of the institution. Illich sees that the church is no longer promoting man's free development of his life with God and with his fellowmen. What happened was that religion became a commodity that was mass-produced, according to an industrial mode. The church has become just one more service organization administering a commodity it has made more scarce. Thus the value of true religion is destroyed; man's freedom is eliminated; human brotherhood has become impossible; a professional elite has developed to control the lives of the people.

Illich does not argue for the elimination of religion, but he does argue for the deinstitutionalization of the church. For him this means a limited church, a small church, one where true religion can be practiced. He desires a community that can maintain the traditions of the past. Religion is to be the activity of a small group of people who are of one mind. He asserts the fundamental freedom of the human person to live out his religious life in total freedom in community with a number of like individuals. He speaks little of the leadership of this community, appearing to accept the Reformation doctrine of the priesthood of all believers.

At the very heart of Illich's religious vision is a concept of human freedom, equality among men, and true brotherhood. These are the fundamental principles that he brings to bear in his criticism of the schools and ultimately of all institutions of society. It is not stated here that everything that Illich gives as a reason for deschooling can be ascribed directly to his religious vision. He repeats many of the criticisms that other radical critics have made about the schools. But when he gives reasons for proposing deschooling as the fundamental step for achieving the convivial reconstruction, one sees as the bases for his reasons certain convictions about man and the desirable society that stem from his fundamentally religious vision of human freedom, equality, and brotherhood. Compulsory education destroys human freedom, which is God-given; it produces a class society; it prevents true fellowship among men.

In a speech in Lima, Peru, Illich (1972b) gave the clearest expression to the theological assumptions underlying his rejection of modern schooling. He bade his audience to become truly radical and prophetic. They were to follow the Scriptures and to follow Jesus by abandoning the myth of progress. He told them:

> We must expose the pseudo-theology of education as preparation for a life of frustrating consumption. We must remind men that God has created a good world and has given us the power to know and cherish it without the need of an intermediary. We know—it is the experience of all of us—that man grows up and learns in the measure in which he is engaged in personal, intimate— always surprising—intercourse with others in a meaningful environment, whereas he shrinks and shrivels when he is served by officials. (Illich, 1972b, p. 48.)

These words clearly indicate the profoundly religious basis for Illich's belief in a God-given freedom of man to learn what he wants to learn. Religious backing is given for the basic equality among men, which is threatened by schooling and a professional group of teachers. A religious-like fellowship among men is viewed as the desirable type of educational experience and community.

Paulo Freire. Like Illich, Paulo Freire is an educational critic who draws some of the basic assumptions for his criticism of education from his particular religious vision. It would be possible for Illich and Freire to arrive at the same views without their religious vision. But it is evident that their particular religious visions influenced greatly all aspects of their thought. Freire is careful to point out that there are various religious visions that might influence one's educational views. He asserts without much doubt, however, that his particular religious vision is the correct one and that it leads to the correct view of education.

Freire's most complete treatment of the relationship between religion and education is found in "The Educational Role of the Churches in Latin America" (Freire, 1972a), and in "Education, Liberation, and the Church" (Freire, 1973b). In the former article he develops three views of religion and compares them with the types of education to which each view would lead. The *traditionalist* view stresses life in the world to come. It is a view that urges people to "reach transcendence without passing through worldliness" (Freire, 1972a, p. 6). This type of religion fosters the closed society and is instrumental in maintaining the *status quo* even if it is a state of oppression. This religious view has concepts of the world, religion, human beings, and human destiny that promote an education that "will inevitably be quietistic, alienated, and alienating" (Freire, 1972a, p. 7).

The second view of religion, of which Freire is also critical, is the *modernizing* perspective. Freire believes that religion in Latin America is moving in this direction. It is changing some of its practices, restating some of its doctrinal positions, getting more involved in problems in the social, economic, and political orders. But it takes only halfway measures that do not bring about the truly radical changes that are necessary. Modernizing religion has its own perspective on education. While it speaks of a liberating education, it stresses only a change in techniques, a change in individuals, rather than the drastic reforms of society that are necessary. This kind of education "means no more than liberating the pupils from their blackboards, from passive classes and bookish curricula;

it means just providing slide projectors and other visual aids, dynamic class plans and technico-professional instruction" (Freire, 1972a, p. 11). It would appear that liberating education is much tamer than modernizing religion—modernizing religion takes a more radical approach to problems in society.

Freire's view of religion is the *prophetic* view. It commits itself to the dominated classes and seeks to transform society radically (Freire, 1972a, p. 11). It refuses to separate concerns for this world from concerns about transcendence. It defines salvation in more worldly terms. For many, this view means recognizing the necessity of violent political revolution (Freire, 1972a, p. 12). Education according to this religious view "will always be . . . a mode of action meant to change things, a political program for the permanent liberation of man" (Freire, 1972a, p. 14). Freire makes this statement about the nature of the prophetic view of education:

> From the prophetic point of view, the specific subject matter of education is of little importance: whatever the subject matter, education is always an effort to understand better something that is concrete. As they focus on it together, the educator-educatee and the educatee-educator will be joined in a creative, active presence, in a clarifying praxis that, as it unveils the reality of awareness, will help to unveil the awareness of reality, too. (Freire, 1972a, p. 14.)

In this rather clumsy and overly rationalized description, Freire seems to indicate that this type of education must include a political program for bringing about objective and radical changes of the structures of society.

Freire's present position with the World Council of Churches has afforded him the opportunity to develop more fully the relationships that exist between his theological and educational views. In an interview in 1970 (Freire, 1970f), Freire spoke of his desire to work with theologians to explore the relationships between a theology for liberation and an education for liberation.

It is clear then that both Illich and Freire appeal to their religious visions in making their criticisms of the schools and of education. An appeal to the prophetic is an appeal to a strong tradition in asserting human rights. Such an appeal has often been made by reformers in all ages. There is, however, a serious problem in setting oneself up as a prophet. It is the tremendous burden of convincing others that one speaks the "word of the Lord." It is always difficult to distinguish the true from the false prophets. One must beware of the person who wears the mantle of the prophet to gain acceptance for his own ideas.

Neither Illich nor Freire avoids this pitfall. Often they speak in an authoritative way without attempting to give arguments for their positions. Often their style of writing becomes sermonic and exhortatory. There is an air of certainty that can be traced to the religious convictions that inspire them in their analyses and directives.

One way to compare the educational criticism of Freire and Illich is to examine three fundamental ideals that they propose for man and society. These ideals have been part of the revolutionary tradition since the French Revolution: liberty, equality, and fraternity. Many of the criticisms that both men make of the schools can be grouped around these concepts, which arise chiefly from the religious vision and tradition which they embrace.

Liberty: Ivan Illich

Illich expresses his concept of freedom to learn in an article entitled "After Deschooling, What?" (Illich, 1971a). In this article he states that only those institutional arrangements should be set up "that protect the autonomy of the learner —his private initiative to decide what he will learn and his inalienable right to learn what he likes rather than what is useful to somebody else" (Illich, 1971a, p. 5). Petrie (1970, p. 473) sees this as one of the four basic principles in Illich's thought. It might be expressed in this manner: We clearly do not have the right to tell another what he must learn, even for his own good.

Illich's statement of the individual's freedom to learn is similar to the statement that anarchists have made concerning the individual's freedom in society. Spring (1973, p. 217) has examined the neglected anarchistic tradition in education, and finds parallels with it in the writings of Illich. Anarchists object to national systems of schooling, for in such systems individual autonomy is severely limited by being directly controlled by the state.

While Illich's expression of human autonomy bears some resemblances to anarchistic concepts of freedom, Illich is clearly no anarchist. He does not call for the abolition of the state, but merely wants to restrict its authority. He accepts the democratic principles of government. A later work (1973b) presents the strongest possible case for the notion that law is a necessary framework for the life of society. Illich shares with many anarchists an equal distaste for American capitalism and Russian Communism. He also shares their liking for the small community and their dislike for bureaucracies. Illich appears to be coming closer to the position of socialists, though he wants to avoid excesses in state socialism as found in Russia.

Illich's principle of freedom to learn does not entail the elimination of institutions, for he himself proposes institutions that can replace our present schools. This is further evidence that he is not an anarchist. Illich believes institutions can exist in society that enhance man's opportunities for free and spontaneous expression.

Illich nowhere offers an argument for his statement that the individual has an inalienable right to learn what he wants to learn. He places the burden of proof on the opposition. One can argue against Illich that we are surely justified in interfering with a child's freedom to learn if we are sure that he is learning something that is harmful to him. Illich would probably admit that we are justified in interfering in order to aid him. He would deny, however, that we can offer sufficient justification for compelling him to attend school. The question comes down to what grounds are sufficient for compelling someone to learn something even if it is against his will.

It is Illich's contention that grounds no longer exist for compulsory education. He argues that schools have passed their second watershed because of the pressure for more and better conditioning of people in the name of education (Illich, 1973b, p. 64). According to Illich's general theory of institutional development, it can be deduced that there was a time when education, though compulsory, was justified because of the good that was accomplished for the individual and for society (Illich, 1973b, p. 7). Schools were once effective tools for providing education, but they no longer are because of the side effects of compulsory schooling: professionalization, social control, myths, and illusions. A CIDOC publication, edited by Jordan Bishop and Joel Spring (1970) supplies the historical evidence for some of Illich's views on compulsory education.

From Illich's own writings, then, it appears that his principle is not an absolute. Interference in the learning of another individual is justified under certain conditions. Recent writings (1973a, 1973b) point to changes in Illich's views of the rights of learners as he begins to consider what deschooling would bring about in society. Contemplating the cost efficiency movement in education, together with the present tendencies toward behavioristic methods in education, Illich (1973b) has been driven to a backhanded compliment to the schools:

> Although the school is destructive and quite inefficient, its traditional character protects at least some rights of the pupil. Educators freed from the restraint of schools could be much more effective and deadly conditioners. (1973b, p. 60.)

Illich began to fear for his deschooling program when he realized that one of the alternatives to public schools would be something like performance contracting—education on the open market. Suddenly, the traditional school began to appear to him as the lesser of two evils. It appears better than "the epoch of the global schoolhouse that would be indistinguishable only in name from a global madhouse or global prison in which education, correction, and adjustment become synonymous" (Illich, 1972a, pp. 241/32). Illich's vision of such a free market in education is for him a nightmare in which "education provides the alchemist with innumerable hidden hands to fit each man into the multiple, tight little niches a more complex technocracy can provide" (Illich, 1972a, pp. 241/15).

Liberty: Paulo Freire

Freire's call to revolution is made also in the name of freedom. But in his case, he does not focus attention on the compulsory nature of the schools. His criticism is aimed more at the process of education, which he terms "banking education" (Freire, 1970a, pp. 57ff.). Such education is an act of depositing; students receive, file, and store deposits. Knowledge is viewed as a gift bestowed on students by the teacher. This type of education offends the humanity and the freedom of the students. Freire proposes, instead, his liberating education. In liberating education, students are on equal terms with their teachers in developing the problems that are to be investigated. They are also free during the entire educational process.

Cultural action for freedom is the expression that Freire uses to designate the educational process itself. This action is one in which a group of people, through dialogue, come to realize the concrete situation in which they exist, the reasons for this situation, and possible solutions. In order for action to be authentic, the participants must be free to create the curriculum along with the teacher (Freire, 1971, p. 114).

Critical Evaluation of the Concept of Liberty

A contradiction in Freire's thought concerning freedom has already been mentioned. He protests that all individuals in the process of education must be free, but when he speaks of his pedagogy for the revolution, he agrees with the ideas of some revolutionaries who have curtailed human freedom in order to advance the cause of the revolution. One can also question whether Freire's students were able to exercise true freedom in their discussions of the problems within their culture. Many appear unconvinced that Freire's methods are truly as respectful of human freedom as he maintains (Weaver, 1972, p. 4; Stanley, 1972, p. 41).

Both Freire and Illich begin with the liberal presumption that human freedom is to be favored. What one does not see presented in their thought is a clear discussion of the grounds on which this presumption in favor of human freedom must yield to other rights and responsibilities. When Freire countenances the restriction on human freedom of those who oppose the revolution, he in fact establishes a broad exception to the principle of freedom: one is permitted to restrain the freedom of those who oppose the plan of action that the leaders of the revolution believe to be the correct action. On this type of reasoning, the former oppressors can be justified in restricting the freedom of those who are attempting to change social, political, and economic policies in the country.

Illich's treatment of human freedom is also inadequate. Illich (1973b) argues for extensive limitations to be placed on the freedom of individuals: consumers, teachers, doctors, businessmen, corporation managers, and such. These limits, which involve many people, are to be placed as the result of due procedures in order to avoid the impending catastrophe. Illich softens the impact of these restrictions by speaking more about the tools that are limited rather than the limitation of the freedom of individuals who use these tools. What his program amounts to, however, is massive restrictions placed upon the freedom of some individuals in order to promote the common good of society.

It is hard to see how Illich can maintain his sweeping concept of freedom to learn in the face of such broad restrictions on human freedom. The amount of compulsion in Illich's convivial society would far exceed the compulsion in any modern society. Illich underestimates this compulsion by prophesying that people will somehow rationally recognize and accept the limits that must be placed on all human institutions. Illich tends to see society as an amorphous public of separate individuals rather than a collective of many competing groups.

In Illich's convivial society it would be necessary to interfere with a person's freedom to learn. Individuals would have to be taught what the proper limits to growth are, and taught not to exceed these limits. Illich places great reliance on the law to bring about his convivially constructed society, and maintain it. But the law could certainly not work alone to maintain order. Educational efforts would be necessary to accompany it, and it is difficult to imagine how these efforts would not involve some interference with a person's freedom to learn.

In his more recent writings Illich (1973b) has conceded that a convivial society does not exclude all schools (p. 24). He asserts, however, that the convivial society does "exclude a school system which has been perverted into a compulsory tool, denying privileges to the dropout" (Illich, 1973b, p. 24). There is a slight problem with Illich's thought here because he has already defined a school as compulsory (Illich, 1970, p. 30). His deschooled society now includes schools, but these differ from present schools in that they are not compulsory. It appears that this admission on Illich's part does blunt the radical edge of his criticisms. He no longer maintains that most learning takes place casually, but admits that what is needed is a proper balance between what can be learned casually and what must be the result of intentional teaching (Illich, 1973b, pp. 57–58).

It is difficult to see how Illich has maintained consistency with his principle of freedom to learn while he calls for a highly controlled society and the admission of schools into this society. This is especially true because Illich totally ignores the overriding issue of classes in society (Rosen, 1972). Schools would appear to be necessary, as Illich admits, to educate people to the proper limits and uses of tools. Illich attempts to maintain his freedom principle by insisting that such schools would not be compulsory. To this it could be replied that the traditional arguments for compulsory schools could easily be imagined as valid in such a controlled and limited society. However, even the existence of noncompulsory schools sufficiently restricts the freedom to learn of those who attend the schools. Noncompulsory schools could well have all the dire effects that Illich points out in compulsory schools. Illich does not describe the schools that he has readmitted into his convivial society; but when one considers the type of society it would be, one can be sure that they would be as intent on preserving a way of life in society as traditional schools are. The fact that these schools would be noncompulsory would not appear to sufficiently guarantee that Illich's proposed radical freedom to learn would be safeguarded.

Illich may have come to his principle of noninterference through an interesting route. His constant parallels to religious freedom and religious institutions may have laid a trap for him (Illich, 1973b, p. 51). He likens the person's freedom to learn to his freedom of religion. The latter is not to be infringed by religious institutions just as the former is not to be infringed by educational institutions. One is not free to impose learning on a person just as one is not free to impose religion on a person. Religious institutions once did impose religion on individuals, but today this is viewed as an unwarranted infringement of human freedom. Illich calls for a similar view with regard to a person's right to learn what he wants and how he wants.

The two kinds of infringement on a person's freedom, however, are not comparable. One infringes upon the child's freedom to teach him those things which are clearly necessary for his survival as a human person. No such necessity exists in the case of religion, notwithstanding what some religionists have maintained in the past and may maintain today. In blurring the distinction between these two freedoms, Illich has too facilely enunciated his principle of noninterference in the learning of another.

Interference with a person's freedom to learn can be justified on a number of grounds. It would seem to be justified on Illich's own grounds to bring about and produce the convivial society. Peters' (1966) argument for compulsory schooling would also appear to be an adequate justification:

> Compulsion cannot force people to become educated. But without it, many children would be deprived of their opportunities for entering into their cultural heritage. Such a limitation on freedom can therefore be justified in terms of the interests of the community and the long-term interest of individuals potentially composing it. For matters as important as this cannot be left purely to the good sense of parents. (Peters, 1966, p. 128.)

It appears then that the call to educational revolution in the name of freedom that has been made by Freire, and more especially by Illich, is a radical position which neither scholar has been able to maintain consistently throughout his writings. Scholars differ on just how radical the criticism of Freire and Illich is. Some contend that there is nothing new in their educational criticism and make attempts to explain the notoriety they have received (Greene, 1972; Friedenberg, 1971; Griffith, 1972). Others believe that they have gone beyond the radical critics of the 1970's, especially in the case of Illich (Gross, 1972; Postman, 1972; Rosen, 1972). It is my contention that Illich's criticism is more radical in the sense that he has forced us to question the ease with which we interfere with another's freedom to learn, and more importantly, he has stretched the imaginations of many to try to conceive of a society without schools. Freire's criticism of education in the name of freedom would appear far less radical than that offered by Illich.

Equality

Both Freire and Illich criticize the schools in the name of equality. Both men propose an egalitarian ideal for society. They are severely critical of the great disparities that exist in modern societies in the areas of wealth, power, and status. Both men speak out of the context of Latin America, where these disparities are indeed great. But they make it clear in their writings that they see the same injustices in the more developed countries. In his "Violence: A Mirror for Americans," Illich (1969, p. 10) draws parallels between the unjust situations that exist in Latin America, the United States, and Vietnam. Freire (1970b) sees basic inequalities in advanced technological countries, for in these countries a myth is accepted in which technology is "projected as all-powerful, beyond all structures, accessible only to a few privileged men" (p. 37).

When Illich and Freire consider the causes of inequality in society, they place a large part of the blame upon education and the schools. For Illich, it is the schools that perpetuate the class society, act as the selectors of individuals for their places in society, certify people for special roles, declare millions of individuals as dropouts or failures, and afford some people extraordinary power. For Freire, it is the domesticating education that prevents people from seeing the true social reality of their lives, thus forcing them to accept the inequalities in which they exist. Both men severely attack the school as *the* institution of society that prevents the existence of the classless society they propose.

Thus far the criticisms of Freire and Illich do not differ

from criticisms that have been leveled by many North American educators. Historians, philosophers, sociologists, psychologists, and anthropologists have made similar criticisms in recent years. Social reconstructionists in education, and such radical educational critics as Goodman, Postman, and Friedenberg, have made compatible statements.

Before we turn to whether or not there is anything new in these criticisms some things bear repeating for a number of reasons. Freire's criticism of education has had a great impact in Latin America and in other countries of the world. So at least what he has said needed saying there. Illich has caused a greater stir in countries like the United States, Canada, England, France, and Germany. It would appear that what he says at least incites interest. With regard to Freire, it is interesting that some Brazilians in the early 1960's. charged him with lack of originality and dependence on North American educators. Freire's reply (1973a) is worth noting:

> In the campaigns carried out against me . . . it was said that I was not the "inventor of dialogue" (as if I had ever made such an irresponsible affirmation). It was said that I had done "nothing original," and that I had "plagiarized European or North American educators," as well as the author of a Brazilian primer. On the subject of originality, I have always agreed with Dewey, for whom originality does not lie in the "extraordinary and fanciful," but "in putting everyday things to uses which had not occurred to others." (Freire, 1973a, p. 5.)

The reply shows Freire's willingness to accept his unoriginality by using an unoriginal reply.

It appears that a strong case can be made for originality in Illich's approach to achieving equality through the schools. Reconstructionists and radical critics look to making vast changes in the schools in order to use them as instruments to bring about an egalitarian society. Illich contends that a necessary condition for the achievement of an egalitarian society is the elimination of the schools. For him, no changes in society are possible unless schools are eliminated. Schools can never be used to bring about fundamental changes because, by their very nature, they reproduce the given society, separate people into classes, and make some more powerful than others (Illich, 1970, pp. 47–51).

Illich cites Cuba as an instance of the failure of a revolution to produce a classless society because of a failure to deschool. He has praise for many of the social and political changes that have taken place in Cuba. "Yet the Cuban pyramid is still a pyramid" (Illich, 1969, p. 185). He thinks that the Cuban revolution will work, but within limits:

> Which means that Dr. Castro will have masterminded a faster road to a bourgeois meritocracy than those previously taken by capitalists or Bolsheviks. . . . As long as communist Cuba continues to promote obligatory high school completion by the end of this decade, it is, in this regard, institutionally no more promising than fascist Brazil, which has made a similar promise. (Illich, 1969, pp. 184–185.)

Illich asserts that Marxist revolutionaries have not sufficiently analyzed the critical role that the school plays in maintaining the existing society, and consequently have not seriously considered the necessity of deschooling.

Freire, unlike Illich, does not focus his attention upon the schools but looks rather to various forms of adult education to be a primary instrument in achieving a classless society. Education will be the key instrument that will make oppressed peoples aware of the oppressive situation in which they live. This critical awareness of the concrete situation will include a denunciation of the oppressive reality together with an annunciation of a new way of life.

While there are different approaches, Freire and Illich agree on at least two propositions. The first is that education and schooling both bring about and maintain the inequalities that exist in society; and second, it will be through a new form of learning that these inequalities will be eliminated. Both Freire and Illich see their analysis as universally applicable. Freire sees oppression not only in Latin America but also in advanced technological countries. Illich's position is even more sweeping in its statement: all countries, whether capitalist, socialist, or mixed, whether highly industrialized, growing, or primitive, should deschool. As has been pointed out above, Illich is beginning to have second thoughts about his call for total deschooling.

Illich (1972a) is attempting to go beyond the disestablishment of schools to what he terms the deschooling of culture. By this he appears to mean to eliminate from society educational efforts as opposed to self-learning efforts. He opposes open classrooms, the free schools, voucher plans, and certification through testing. These are opposed because they not only interfere with the individual's right to learn what he wants and prevent him from doing for himself what he can truly do, but they also can be utilized to maintain the forms of privilege and power that are at the foundation of a society with established classes.

Illich stated that this cited article would be his last writing on education. He has not been entirely faithful to this statement, for he has returned to the schools in a later book, *Tools for Conviviality*. Illich asserted in a lecture at CIDOC in July 1972 that the key problem for deschoolers in the future would be to work out the problem he has pinpointed: that disestablishment of schools would lead to a take-over of educational functions in society by institutions, which would more effectively hamper human freedom and promote even greater inequality (unpublished lecture at which the author was present).

It appears from *Tools for Conviviality* that Illich has not left this problem to others but has made some attempts at a solution. As has been shown above, he admits that all schools would not necessarily be eliminated from a convivial society. It only excludes those schools at which attendance is compulsory. Also, all education through teaching is not to be eliminated, but what must be maintained is a proper balance between self-learning and learning through teaching. In the following chapter the nature of the educational institutions that Illich permits into his convivial society will be examined.

In *Tools for Conviviality,* Illich appears to hold his original position that the disestablishment of compulsory schools is a necessary condition for an egalitarian society. But he does give more attention to all the other changes that must take place if such a society would be achieved. He also admits that some inequality will exist in the convivial society, but he gives no adequate treatment of the grounds on which it might be justified (Illich, 1973b, p. 1).

It was stated earlier that both men view education and the schools as the chief instruments for establishing and maintaining the classist society with its many inequalities. Illich contends that such is the case in all societies of the world. He also contends that schools are helpless to remedy the situation. Freire, however, presents his liberating pedagogy as an instrument for achieving the revolution that would bring about the classless society. Neither Illich nor Freire offers much empirical evidence for his assertions, and much is needed. Freire's position can be accommodated to the views of social reconstructionists in education. His views differ from these thinkers in that his major focus is not upon the schools but rather upon adult or community education. Illich's proposal for deschooling, is closer in some aspects to certain anarchist educators, though in his later writings he has moved closer to socialist thought.

Fraternity

The third revolutionary principle which both Illich and Freire advocate is fraternity. Their criticisms of the schools and of education are made in the name of fraternity. Fraternity is used here to embrace the quality of the relationship that should exist among men in society. It is held to represent a certain equality of social esteem, the absence of manners of deference and servility, and a sense of civic friendship and social solidarity (Rawls, 1971, p. 105). The ideal of fraternity involves bonds of sentiment and feeling. True fraternity exists in society when its institutions enrich the personal and social lives of its citizens (Rawls, 1971, p. 107). Both Illich and Freire see present educational arrangements as militating against true fraternity.

Religious Roots of This Concept. For both Illich and Freire, the ideal of fraternity has obvious religious roots and overtones. Illich's proposed church of the future would embrace "intimate familial celebrations of conversion to the gospel in the milieu of the home" (Illich, 1969, p. 63). He has called for declericalization so that the "periodic meeting of friends would replace the Sunday assembly of strangers" (Illich, 1969, p. 82). In a later article, Illich (1972c, p. 18) argued that one of the basic problems with the Catholic Church today is its tendency to see itself as a state or political entity, or an industrial and service institution. He proposes a structure of the church that would "create an atmosphere of freedom in which people who want to approach the Lord know that they can celebrate the encounter with the 'other' in a very traditional and, therefore, very trivial form which is itself always open to the new" (Illich, 1972c, p. 21).

Freire speaks often of the "communion" that should exist among men in society. This word has deep religious meanings within the Christian faith, referring to the Christian's spiritual and symbolic union with Jesus and also to the spiritual union that exists among members of the Christian faith. For Freire, fraternal solidarity is essential for religious, political, and educational salvation or liberation. He makes the parallel himself:

> Men free themselves only in concert, in communion, collaborating on something wrong that they want to correct. There is an interesting theological parallel to this: no one saves another, no one saves himself all alone,

because only in communion can we save ourselves or not save ourselves. (Freire, 1972c, p. 8.)

As Rawls (1971, p. 105) points out, it is not easy to separate the demands for fraternity from the demands for freedom and equality in society. This becomes apparent when Illich's and Freire's criticisms of education are investigated on these grounds. Yet there appear to be charges that both men make against modern educational institutions that can be gathered under this rubric.

Illich's Critique. Illich's criticisms of the schools in the name of fraternity can be made briefly. Schools prevent "the meeting among people who share an issue, which for them at the moment is socially, intellectually, and emotionally important" (Illich, 1970, p. 18). Schools prevent true fraternity between children and adults by maintaining children in a state of deference for a long period of their lives (Illich, 1970, pp. 26–28). Through the process of schooling, children are given a sense of their own inferiority. It is the poor especially who lose self-esteem through schooling. Schools favor the rich, whom family and culture have prepared for the experience, while the poor are further disadvantaged by being declared misfits or dropouts (Illich, 1970, p. 29). True fraternity does not exist within schools, for these institutions exercise the roles of custodian, preacher, and therapist. Too great a deference is given to teachers; teachers pry into the private affairs of their students (Illich, 1970, pp. 31–32). Through the schooling process, students become much more susceptible to accept all types of rankings in society which are adverse to true fraternity and civic friendship (Illich, 1970, p. 40). Schooling produces alienation among students by conditioning them to value those things which one receives from institutions while assigning less value to those things which are done out of a spirit of independence and relatedness to others (Illich, 1970, p. 47). Educational bureaucracies prevent the development of the personal and social lives of students.

One type of learning institution that Illich proposes, peer matching, is especially designed to inculcate in society this spirit of fraternity (Illich, 1970, p. 96).

The ideal of fraternity is at the heart of Illich's plan for convivial reconstruction. He intends conviviality to mean "autonomous and creative intercourse among persons, and the intercourse of persons with their environment . . . individual freedom realized in personal interdependence" (Illich, 1973b, p. 11). Only those educational institutions can be admitted into the convivial society which foster this ideal of conviviality. Schools as presently constituted in all countries of the world do not promote this ideal. This lack of true fraternity within the schools is at the heart of the oppressive industrial system in both capitalist and socialist countries. According to Illich (1973b), students

> learn to value grade advancement, passive submission, and even the standard misbehavior that teachers like to interpret as a sign of creativity. They learn disciplined competition for the favor of the bureaucrat who presides over their daily sessions, who is called their teacher as long as they are in class and their boss when they go to work. . . . They learn to accept their places in society precisely in the class and career corresponding to the level at which they leave school and to the field of their academic specialization. (Illich, 1973b, p. 62.)

Illich remains convinced that at the basis of all societal problems lies the school, the essential institution for maintaining all present societies. The building of true fraternity must start with the deschooling of society.

Freire's Critique. Freire's critique of education in the developing countries, like Illich's, is governed by an ideal of fraternity which he considers essential to a democratic society. In these countries, an authoritarian education maintained "a rigidly authoritarian structure of life, which formed and strengthened an antidemocratic mentality" (Freire,

1973a, p. 26). Freire criticized Brazilian education for its lack of faith in the student and his power to discuss, work, and create. The Brazilian tradition, he asserts, was not one of working *with* the students, but one of working *on* them (Freire, 1973a, p. 38). Freire lays the failure of efforts for democratic reform in Brazil at the feet of the type of relationship that exists in Brazilian society, particularly the master-slave relationship analyzed by Freyre (1964). This type of relationship still exists between teacher and student (Freire, 1973a, pp. 27ff.). Such an authoritative social organization prevents the necessary development of a sense of fraternity essential for bringing about the democratic society.

Freire's attack on "banking education" is shaped by the ideal of fraternity that he espouses. "Banking education" offends true fraternity because, according to Freire, the teacher is the subject of the learning process, while the pupils are mere objects (Freire, 1970a, p. 59). It is the teacher who teaches, knows everything, disciplines, chooses, has authority. The pupil is in a position of subservience and must pay deference to the teacher (Freire, 1970a, pp. 59–60). The student is not admitted to true partnership in learning in this form of education (Freire, 1970a, p. 62). No solidarity exists between teacher and pupils because there is no true communication upon which solidarity is based. This type of education "stimulates the credulity of students, with the ideological intent (often not perceived by educators) of indoctrinating them to adapt to the world of oppression" (Freire, 1970a, p. 65). To the banking form of education, Freire opposes his problem-posing education which is based upon respect, communication, and solidarity. This type of education promotes that spirit of fraternity which is essential to a truly democratic education for a democratic society.

Freire's application of the principle of fraternity in his educational criticism does not lead him to embrace the "human relations" movement or sensitivity training in education. His reason for not espousing this movement is interesting:

The techniques of "human relations" are not the answer, for in the final analysis they are only another way of domesticating and alienating men even further in the service of greater productivity. (Freire, 1970b, p. 50.)

DeWitt (1971) takes issue with Freire by contending:

Insights into the dynamics of human relationships yielded by investigations of social scientists can be intelligently and systematically acted upon to effect rational social change. (DeWitt, 1971, p. 192.)

Hampden-Turner (1971) has also argued for the value of T-groups for effective radical social change.

While both Illich and Freire utilize the principle of fraternity in their criticism of the schools and education, there are differences in their utilizations of it. Illich makes the point that modern schools, by the very nature of their connection with industrial and consumer society, perpetuate a society in which some persons are necessarily servile in their relationships to others, in which many persons lack sufficient self-esteem, and in which civic friendship is rendered impossible by an excessively competitive ethos. The first step to take in order to foster true fraternity is to abolish the schools, for the school, according to Illich, is the crucial institution which maintains the existing manipulative societies. Freire, on the other hand, looks more deeply into the teacher-student relationship. He is less concerned with the institution in which this relationship is found. He sees this relationship as paternalistic in nature, mirroring as it does the relationships that exist elsewhere in Brazilian society. The analyses by the two appear to be complementary.

Radical critics of North American schools have made similar criticisms of the schools (Friedenberg, 1963; Goodman, 1969). Historians have shown the paternalistic pattern to be a pervasive one in the history of education in the United States (Greer, 1972; Katz, 1968). Freire's views are somewhat akin to Dewey's democratic conception of education (Dewey, 1917). Illich's point is more radical; it is also more difficult to substantiate. The school would not appear to be so crucial as Illich thinks for maintaining modern industrial society. Rosen (1972) makes the point:

> The American industrial empire came to maturity and power without the active collaboration of the sort of school system that Illich makes his primary target. Our present concentrations of wealth and power protect and extend themselves in many ways, of which the school may be the most easily dispensed with. (Rosen, 1972, p. 44.)

The first part of Rosen's statement—that the American industrial empire came to maturity without active collaboration of the schools—is open to serious question because of the research conducted by Spring (1972). It appears that Rosen is more on target with his statement that the continued existence of the American industrial empire does not depend upon the existence of the schools. Bowles (1972) and Raskin (1972) have both argued that changing the schools will not have much effect on the dominant economic, social, and political institutions of American society.

The survival of the school system would not appear to be crucial for the survival of industrial society. Berg (1970) has shown that industry can do with much less schooling for its future workers. Workers, technicians, and consumers can be captured in other ways, such as the mass media and advertising. The economic and political powers in America have not been greatly concerned with the crisis of learning that exists in urban areas. The failures in the American work force would also be a welcome excuse to shift production away from urban areas and even into foreign countries.

In this chapter, I have explained the essential criticisms that Freire and Illich have made of schooling and education. This is the negative aspect of their criticisms. What remains to be considered is the constructive aspect of their educational theory.

6

Educational Theorists

With this chapter, we come to the very heart of the educational theories of Freire and Illich. Important aspects of the explicitly stated educational theories of these two contemporary thinkers will be examined. Illich and Freire have been presented thus far as existential Christian humanists, preachers of revolutions, and educational critics. Both men are clearly utopian thinkers attracted to the socialist ideal of man and society. What remain to be discussed are the educational theories they have developed from these assumptions and the concrete proposals they make for educational reform. A comparison will be made of their thought in these areas. A criticism of their major theories and proposals will also be presented.

The task of explaining the positive educational philosophy of Freire and Illich is not easy. Like most utopian thinkers, they are much clearer critics and more precise in what they reject in contemporary educational theories and practices than they are in stating constructive options. Vagueness and generality set in when they make positive proposals and attempt to describe what education or learning should be in utopian societies. However, there are sufficient indications in their writings of their positive thought to develop their essential ideas in this area.

The educational theories of both Illich and Freire easily fit into the mold of normative or prescriptive theories. A normative philosophy of education, according to Frankena

(1970), includes statements about aims, principles, and methods of a normative character; some data of empirical fact; and metaphysical, epistemological, or theological assumptions. (Frankena, 1970, p. 16). Thus the educational theories of Freire and Illich differ from the analytic approach to educational philosophy, which has become most prevalent in the English-speaking world. One finds in their writings some attempts at the analysis of concepts, but this is clearly secondary to the normative statements they make about education, learning, schools, aims, content, and methods. They are clearly concerned with what education and schools should or should not be.

Illich's Theory of Learning

At the heart of his educational theory, Illich places his notion of what learning should be. In a dialogue at the Center for the Study of Democratic Institutions, Illich was forced to admit the harm that the disestablishment of schools might lead to. He recognized that it could open the way to a conscious engineering of people and society as happens in totalitarian societies. His daring response to this awareness is interesting enough to quote in full. He states that he "feels very badly about this whole thing frequently."

> I know that our criticism is destructive of one of the great creations of the last two generations. It pulls the rug out from under the only ritual which at this moment keeps stability. It calls for a radical alternative which we cannot imagine, because I do not know how one imagines the sense of the future. It therefore opens the gates in a very much more subtle way than a politician would do to something as horrible as Jacobinism. The ideas which we profess about education are no less dangerous than the political ideas of the Enlightenment. I think *the whole argument stands and falls on our understanding of learning.* If learning be the product of a treatment, we would end up with the totally taught society, which

almost necessarily leads to Vietnam. (Illich, 1971c, p. 7; italics added.)

Illich has to some degree modified his views on the deschooling of society as he has contemplated what would be the realistic consequences of such a drastic change. Nonetheless, the concept of learning remains the critical point on which his theory rests. In every book, article, and talk, he comes back again and again to a view of what human learning should be.

The social philosophy that Illich espouses advocates a society in which there is maximum individual freedom, complete equality among men in society, and extensive opportunities for the promotion of fraternity in society. It has been shown that an important source of his social philosophy is his particular view of the Christian tradition. In his Beecher Lectures at Yale, Illich (1971b, p. 5/21) asserts his agreement with those who point out that the schools do harm to individuals in bringing about their loss of freedom and in producing conformity and docility. He himself, however, wants to underline the cancerous social effects of schools. Universal obligatory education sets men against men and nations against nations. Schools are discriminatory and degrading. Schools manipulate the contact between the child and his environment. Illich's distinction between the social and individual effects is not sharp, for conformity might well be considered both an individual and a social effect of schooling.

The type of learning Illich espouses is one that promotes human freedom, equality, and fraternity. True learning is learning in which a person freely consents to participate. Illich asserts that no one has the right to interfere in the learning of another without his consent. He makes the empirical claim, for which he offers little substantiation, that most learning is not the result of teaching, but rather is gathered incidentally as one participates in life. The learnings which a person cannot gather incidentally from life and things, he can easily appropriate from a skill master, a peer, or from books and other learning instruments.

For Illich, then, the fundamental aspect of true learning is that it is freely chosen learning from life, both from things and from persons. Compulsory learning is always harmful to the individual and to society. Illich believes that incidental learning should be greater than what is learned as a result of intentional teaching (Illich, 1973b, p. 57). Tools, machines, technology should be developed in such a way that they can be easily utilized by persons working on their own. Simple tools in society will eliminate the necessity for a knowledge elite that have excessive power by reason of their knowledge of the working of the tools and institutions of society.

Illich's espousal of total freedom in education and opposition to all forms of compulsion in learning is at the very heart of his social and educational theories. It is in some ways an anarchistic position. Many have associated Illich's views in this regard with the educational philosophy of Rousseau. Though some valid comparisons can be made between these two theorists, there exist wide differences between them when one looks beyond the *Emile* (Boyd, 1962a) to the educational writings of Rousseau which advocate national education (Boyd, 1962b). In these writings, Rousseau favored state control over education that entailed indoctrination into the ideals of the national state. It has been shown in this book that Illich's convivial society might demand great restrictions on human freedom for its full implementation.

A more accurate comparison might be made with the educational theory of Tolstoy (Tolstoy, 1967). One finds many of Illich's ideas in the writings of this nineteenth-century Christian anarchist who opposed the adoption of compulsory education in Russia. Tolstoy contended that no one has the right to educate another against his will. Like Illich, he sang the lavish praises of incidental education (Tolstoy, 1967, pp. 145ff.). He advocated the kind of skill-training that Illich espouses (p. 139). Tolstoy manifested the same antiprogress attitudes that have become most prevalent in Illich's later writings (pp. 166ff.). Tolstoy anticipated Illich's contention that modernization does not benefit the working classes but rather the upper classes of society.

Illich makes rather extensive claims for the freedom to learn which he espouses. He contends that educational research has demonstrated that children learn most of what teachers pretend to teach them from peer groups, chance observations, and comics (Illich, 1970, p. 29). Freedom to learn will result in immeasurable re-creation of knowledge and unlimited opportunity for meeting among people who share an issue which for them is socially important (Illich, 1970, p. 18). Free learning will enable persons to be spontaneous, independent, and interrelated to one another (Illich, 1970, p. 52). This type of learning will increase man's poetic ability, his power to endow the world with his personal meaning, and his creative energies (Illich, 1973b, pp. 60ff.). Bell (1973, pp. 419–422) rightly criticizes Illich for anti-intellectualism on the ground that Illich fails to make an adequate distinction between experience and knowledge.

The two basic claims that Illich makes about free learning must be examined. First of all, he makes the empirical claim that most learning is not the result of teaching but is, rather, casual in nature. As Petrie (1972) notes, this is quite a sweeping claim and one that is very difficult to prove or disprove (p. 472). Petrie does not examine this claim directly, but rather attempts to indicate the new perspective that Illich opens up through this claim: that compulsory schooling of its very nature leads to knowledge harmful to both man and society. Petrie's discussion of this point adds little to Illich's claim except to make more explicit the meaning that Illich has intended (Petrie, 1972, p. 473).

Illich's espousal of incidental learning as the predominant mode of learning is modified somewhat in his later writings. In *Tools for Conviviality* (1973b, pp. 58ff.), he calls for a proper balance between learning that is a result of intentional teaching and learning that can be learned from ordinary life. He states that the balance of learning should be skewed in favor of spontaneous and convivial learning (Illich,

1973b, pp. 55ff.). Such a modification would appear to be called for in the convivial society that he proposes since this society would demand a rather controlled type of existence not favorable to excessive spontaneous learning on the part of its citizens.

It appears from this modification that Illich is less strong in his claim for incidental learning. This claim would appear secondary, however, to his overall thesis. His chief targets are the school systems which he believes perpetuate the existences of those societies which he opposes. He is against the type of learning that goes on in these schools, for this learning aids in maintaining the existing societies. He does not think these systems can be reformed, and thus he is forced to praise incidental learning which he views as the alternative to school learning.

The best reply to Illich on this matter is given, it appears, by one who in some ways admires his thought. Jonathan Kozol has visited Cuernavaca on a number of occasions. Yet, he tells us, he is less impressed with the Illich-Reimer view when he returns to the realities of the Boston ghetto. Kozol (1972) writes:

> It is a luxury at 2,000 miles' distance to consider an educational experience that does not involve credentials or curriculum, or long-term sequential learning. In immediate terms, in cities such as Boston and New York, it is unwise and perhaps destructive to do so. Instead, we must face up to the hard truth that these credentials and measured areas of expertise and certified ability constitute as of now, the irreducible framework of our labor and struggle. (Kozol, 1972, p. 33.)

Kozol's point is that millions of people in the cities of the United States are without the survival skills which Illich has contended are picked up incidentally. Kozol contends that these survival skills are desperately important for the children of the powerless in our society. Katz (1971, p. 145) and Havighurst (1971, p. 90) are also hesitant about abolishing compulsory education because of the harm this would do to the poor. Illich's argument would probably be that this society must be changed and the first step must be the disestablishment of schools. He would see Kozol's approach, as doomed to failure in the long run. But who can afford to be concerned with the long run?

Illich has done well to bring to our attention the values of free, incidental, and noncompulsory education. Others have done this before, notably Rousseau, the nineteenth-century naturalists, and in our century, Paul Goodman. Educators need constantly to be reminded that school learning constitutes only a part of learning. They need often be reminded of some of the unsavory aspects of school learning as Illich and others, notably Robert Dreeben (1968), have pointed out. Yet Illich's excessive claims for free learning must be countered with the pragmatic stance of an educational practitioner who tells us that what Harlem needs is "radical, strong, subversive, steadfast, rage-minded, and power-wielding obstetricians, pediatricians, lab technicians, defense attorneys, building code examiners, and brain surgeons" (Kozol, 1972, p. 114).

Illich's second principle is that no one has the right to interfere in the learning of another. Illich contends that we clearly do not have the right to tell another what he must learn, even for his own good. It is Illich's conviction that the burden of proof for interfering in the life of another is placed on the one who interferes. He views compulsory schooling as an unjust interference with the rights of the individual. He calls for a constitutional amendment guaranteeing this right (Illich, 1972b, p. 55).

This second principle of Illich is based on the first principle and its presuppositions. Since most learning is of a casual nature, and since school learning leads to harmful effects on the individual and society, then it is claimed that there is no right to impose compulsory schooling on individuals. What Illich sees most harmful about school is that people through attending school become addicted consumers in society.

Through induction into the ritual of school, a person becomes addicted to more school learning, prizing this learning not for itself, but rather for the benefits it grants to the person who has been certified through the schools. The person is then inclined to look for his real benefits from institutions in society.

One can readily grant to Illich the great value of learning that is freely chosen by the individual. The element of motivation is strong. One can also grant that Illich has touched an important point when he claims that the right of interference must be proved on the part of the person who teaches. In all societies, the burden of proof is on the students if they want to deviate from the rules of the teacher, school, and society. Educators have been more concerned with the rights of parents, society, and themselves, forgetting the rights of students in this matter. Compulsory education laws have been too rigidly enforced against the rights of individuals and other institutions of society. Until recently, in fact, children have had no legal rights in the United States.

With his second principle Illich brings up the issue that must be faced by educators in every era. This issue, which has been especially pronounced since the Enlightenment, is the moral justification of compulsory schooling. Schooling is obviously an infringement upon the freedom of the child. This freedom is justifiably infringed, it seems, for the benefit of the child and for the benefit of society. Illich comes closer to this position in *Tools for Conviviality* (1973b) as he begins to contemplate what the alternatives to deschooling would be and when he admits schools of a noncompulsory nature into the convivial society. Illich is guilty of exaggerating the achievements of the schools in perpetuating the existing society. Bereiter (1972), in an article somewhat favorable to the Illich-Reimer position, reports on research in this area. A review of published research led him to the conclusion that "while schooling had a demonstrable effect on certain skills, on the acquisition of organized bodies of knowledge, and on critical thinking abilities, it apparently had no demonstrable effects on productive thinking abilities, personality traits, attitudes and values, or citizenship" (Bereiter, 1972, p. 32). The heart of Illich's argument for totally free learning lies in the deleterious effects he ascribes to compulsory schooling. No evidence can be adduced to support his contention that any and all schools produce the harm that he ascribes to them. Noncompulsory learning cannot be supported on these grounds.

Illich's advocacy of totally free learning has involved him in the paradox of freedom. Too great freedom will lead to repression. It may lead to the developments of educational institutions more successful than schools in molding their clients. It may leave millions of children within the narrow confines of their own and their families' interests. Peters (1966) has spoken well of this paradox of freedom when he notes:

> If people are allowed to do what they like, what tends to happen is that the strong impose arbitrary constraints on the weak. In such spheres, individuals are only in fact free to do or say what they like if they are protected from arbitrary interference by law or public opinion or both. The unpalatable lesson of history is that it takes a constraint to catch a constraint. (Peters, 1966, p. 110.)

Other weaknesses are also found in Illich's treatment of learning. He never considers the possibility of a person's learning false things through incidental learning. Also, he almost totally ignores various kinds of learning that have been analyzed by philosophers of education (Komisar, 1967, pp. 211–223). Illich nowhere treats the varying types of relationships that exist between teachers and students corresponding to the various types of learning.

Freire's Theory of Learning

If learning is the crucial concept in Illich's educational theory, conscientization is the heart of Freire's educational theory. In the past ten years, Freire has been associated more with this term than has any other Latin-American educator. Freire tells us that the word was born during a series of round-table meetings of professors at the Brazilian Institute of Higher Studies in 1964. Freire does not know exactly who coined the term, but he tells us that when he heard it, he became fully convinced that "education, as an exercise in freedom, is an act of knowing, a critical approach to reality. It was inevitable that the word became a part of the terminology I used thereafter to express my pedagogical views, and it easily came to be thought of as something I had created" (Freire, 1972c, p. 1).

Freire's concept of conscientization was presented in his first book, and he has added little to the concept since. In later writings he has dealt rather extensively with explaining what knowing is from a phenomenological point of view. He has also attached the concept of conscientization to a more radical political philosophy. The basic concept, however, remains the same throughout his works.

In *Education for Critical Consciousness,* Freire (1973a) speaks of conscientization as the development of critical awareness achieved through dialogical educational programs concerned with social and political responsibilities (Freire, 1973a, p. 19). The purpose of this process is to bring about critical attitudes in people. These critical attitudes are to lead to the transformation of the world (1973a, p. 34). He calls this democratic education, for it is founded on faith in man, on the belief that men not only can discuss the problems of their country but also have the power to solve these problems (1973a, p. 38). Conscientization includes exchange of ideas, debates, discussions, and working *with* students and not *on* them (p. 38).

In "Extension or Communication," Freire (1973a) speaks of conscientization as resulting from confrontation with the world, as constant researching, as invention and reinvention (1973a, p. 100). It is built upon the relations between human beings and the world, relations of transformation. It perfects itself through placing critical focus on these problems (p.

109). Conscientization for Freire is not an individual but a social task. It is also never neutral, for the educator has the right to have options, but he must not impose them (1973a, pp. 148–149).

In *Pedagogy of the Oppressed,* Freire (1970a) gives a fuller explanation of conscientization. He terms it co-intentional education, in which students and teachers co-intend reality, that is, both are subjects in critically unveiling reality and in re-creating knowledge (Freire, 1970a, pp. 55–56). This form of education receives a more philosophical explanation in this work. Conscientization takes place in

> a learning situation in which the cognizable object (far from being the end of the cognitive act) intermediates the cognitive actors—teachers and students. The student-teacher contradiction must be resolved in order to have dialogic relations, in order to have true education. The teacher is also taught through dialogue with his students. No one teaches another, nor is anyone self-taught. Men teach each other, mediated by the world, by the cognizable objects. (Freire, 1970a, pp. 66–67.)

A similarity exists between Freire's rejection of "banking education" and Illich's distaste for formal education.

Perhaps the best definition of what Freire means by conscientization is contained in an editor's footnote in *Cultural Action for Freedom* (1970b). Conscientization is there defined as "the process in which men, not as recipients, but as knowing subjects, achieve a deepening awareness both of the sociocultural reality which shapes their lives, and of their capacity to transform that reality through action upon it" (Freire, 1970b, p. 27). Freire has shown himself sensitive to the charge that his position is an idealistic one, making it comparable to awareness or the French *prise de conscience.* Freire contends that conscientization goes deeper than this. It goes deeper because it penetrates to what reality really is and because it is connected with praxis. Freire's concept of praxis—social action plus reflection—depends upon the

Marxist concept of praxis (Fromm, 1961, pp. 22ff.; Lefebvre, 1968, pp. 25–58). Conscientization demands a historical commitment; it demands involvement and intervention in reality. For Freire, then, conscientization does not create reality, but merely discovers it. It also implies a real intervention into reality through action. In Marxist terms, which he is fond of using, conscientization entails both the denouncing of an oppressive reality and the announcement of a liberating reality. Sartre (1966) has described the phenomenological thrust as an attempt to avoid idealism and materialism by forging a third way which is both objective and subjective.

Crucial to an understanding of Freire's concept of conscientization is his theory of the various levels of consciousness (1973a). The lowest level of consciousness he calls *intransitive consciousness*. Men at this level are preoccupied with meeting their most elementary needs. They are characterized by the near absence of historical consciousness. Persons at this level are almost impervious to problems and challenges beyond the biological sphere. They are immersed in a one-dimensional oppressive present. The relationships that they have entered have shaped their sociocultural situation and cannot be comprehended by them.

Semi-intransitivity or *magical consciousness* is the second level of consciousness. This type of consciousness is prevalent in the emerging societies of the Third World. It is the prevailing consciousness of closed societies, of the culture of silence. Persons at this level take the facts of their sociocultural situations as "givens." This form of consciousness is characterized by a fatalistic mentality, which views all of life as related to destiny or fortune, forces beyond the control of man. Self-depreciation is a most common attribute of this level of consciousness, for the people have internalized the negative values that the dominant culture ascribes to them. This level of consciousness is also marked by excessive emotional dependence. To be is to be under someone, to depend on him. This form of consciousness often expresses itself in defensive and therapeutic magic.

Naïve or *semitransitive consciousness* is the third level of consciousness. Freire also terms this level *popular conscious-ness.* Silence is not the characteristic of this level. A serious questioning of one's life situation begins, but at a naïve and primitive level. This consciousness is more likely to see the cultural situation as determined by men. People in this stage of development are easily swayed by populist leaders. People begin to sense that they have some control over their lives, but the danger of manipulative populist leadership is ever great.

Before we pass to Freire's highest level of consciousness, it is important to note the obvious Marxist character of this analysis. Like Marx, Freire explains cultural-historical reality as a superstructure in relationship to an infrastructure. Op-pressed class is opposed to oppressing class. The three levels of consciousness of Freire correspond to the false or reifying consciousness of Marx. "Reification" for Marx is the appre-hension of the products of human activity as if they were products of nature, cosmic laws, or divine will. The reified world is a dehumanized world. The real relationship be-tween man and his world is reversed in this consciousness. Man is viewed as the product of a world which he, in fact, has made. Man is capable paradoxically of producing a reality that denies him. In Marxist thought, reification is closely al-lied to alienation (Berger, 1966, pp. 200–201).

The highest level of consciousness for Freire is *critical consciousness,* achieved through the process of conscientiza-tion. This level is marked by depth in the interpretation of problems, self-confidence in discussions, receptiveness, and refusal to shirk responsibility. The quality of discourse here is dialogical. At this level, the person scrutinizes his own thoughts, he sees the proper causal and circumstantial corre-lations. Conscientization for Freire, in the context of Latin America, means a radical denunciation of dehumanizing structures, accompanied by announcement of a new reality to be created by men. It entails a rigorous and rational cri-tique of the ideology that supports these structures. Critical consciousness is brought about not through intellectual efforts alone but through praxis, the authentic union of action and reflection.

At this point a serious weakness in Freire's concept of conscientization can be indicated. Freire almost says that a person's knowledge of his true interests guarantees a person's participation in activity to achieve these interests. As Horowitz (1966) rightly points out:

> The line between action and interests is far from straight. Even if we ignore the dilemmas arising out of a direct correlation of actions and interests, there is a policy issue involved; namely, the degree of social unrest necessary to stimulate a person to think along developmental lines without creating complete revolutionary upheaval. (Horowitz, 1966, p. 295.)

There is the real possibility that people involved in conscientization might become even more entrenched in their thinking once they see the full impact of oppression in their lives.

Having discussed the role of consciousness-raising in Freire's thought, it is possible to see more clearly his theory of human learning. Learning for Freire is the process by which one moves from one level of consciousness to another. The content of each level is the view that one has of existence in the social world and the power that one has to determine one's destiny. Learning begins with assessing the present level of consciousness as it is manifest in language, self-concept, world view, and present living conditions. Becoming aware of the contingency of social reality is the beginning of learning. In other words, learning is the movement toward critical consciousness. Its basis is an awareness that there is an essential difference between the givenness of the natural world and the contingency of the social world. This contingent world lies within the power of man to change. Learning is thus the process of challenging and being challenged by the givenness of one's life situation and of the sociocultural reality in which one lives.

For Freire, learning is predominantly an active process. He is strongly opposed to what he terms the "banking" concept of learning. The process rather begins with the learner's words, ideas, and life situation. The educator uses these to codify the concrete world in which the learner lives. The task of the educator is to aid learners to examine, challenge, and criticize these situations as presented to him verbally and pictorially.

In emphasizing the activity of the learner in the process, Freire is not blazing a new trail. This principle has been repeated often by philosophers and psychologists of education. But his strong emphasis on learning as dialogical action between learners and educators highlights a crucial aspect of social learning. The adult literacy process implies for him the existence of two interrelated contexts:

> One is the context of authentic dialogue between learners and educators as equally knowing subjects. This is what schools should be—theoretical contexts of dialogue. The second is the real, concrete context of facts, the social reality in which men exist. (Freire, 1970b, p. 14.)

There is a close connection between these two contexts. The Marxist concept of praxis as the continuing dialectical relationship between action and reflection bridges the gap between the two contexts. The group reflects on its actions in order to gain a deeper understanding of them and of their causes so that they will be able to act differently according to their new understanding. Learning, for Freire, then, is the total process of becoming aware of the concrete situation in which ones lives, understanding how that situation came about, how it might be changed, and then acting to change it. This conception of learning is similar to Dewey's view of learning as the reconstruction of experience. In Marxist terminology, conscientization is the continuing process of knowing and denouncing one reality and announcing a new reality toward which men can strive.

At this point some major differences between the educational thought of Illich and Freire can be noted. Illich is concerned with the learning of individuals as individuals while Freire is concerned with the learning of individuals as members of a particular group or class (Elias, 1974). Illich is most concerned with the freedom of the individual to pursue his own spontaneous learning. Freire also makes the freedom of the individual essential in his educational philosophy. In practice, however, the individual comes under strong pressure from the group and particularly the coordinator of the group. In fact, the charge of subtle manipulation has been made of the Freire method. Illich considers freedom to learn the central issue in his educational theory, but he has not reconciled his views on this freedom with the demands of the convivial society. Freire, on the other hand, emphasizes the social aspects of human learning. Both men are intent on freeing the individual from dehumanizing and oppressive learning, but it is to Freire rather than to Illich that we look for a description of a nonoppressive form of learning. Illich, however, provides a much more incisive account of the forms of modern oppression about which man ought to be conscientized.

A major contribution of both Freire and Illich is that they are keenly aware of the political nature of learning and knowledge. Illich charges the educational systems in all countries with totally socializing persons for life in a particular social and political system. Freire sees educational systems in the Third World as the chief tools used by oppressive elites to dominate the masses. For both men, learning and knowledge is political because it is power for those who generate it as much as it is for those who use it. It is Freire, however, who analyzes more thoroughly the politics of knowing. For him, to learn or to know something is inseparable from deciding to change it, to preserve it, to destroy it, or to fully experience it as one's own problem.

A Critique of Freire's Theory of Learning. Freire's concept of learning as conscientization can be criticized on a number of points. One criticism has already been made, where Freire has been accused of excessive idealism in his description of conscientization. Another criticism that might be leveled at this theory is its dependence on some sort of transcendent view of reality. Through conscientization, for Freire, individuals are brought to see reality as it really is. In Freire's description of his method, the group arrives at a true and authentic knowledge of the situation. One sees little awareness in his writings of the complexities of the reality with which people are attempting to grapple. In his public addresses and conversations, he appears less certain. It is my view that Freire betrays here another influence of his religious vision, with its absolutes about man and nature. His view of the fixity of man, nature, and the world conflicts with his statements about man's making history and making culture. These later ideas appear to be less rigid in Freire's thought. We may have here an example of the classic difficulty experienced by many Christian thinkers in assimilating some of the dynamic concepts of Marxist thought into their more static notions of religious thought about man and reality.

Still, Freire's concept of learning as conscientization is interesting for a number of reasons. It is refreshing to look at a theory of human learning that has been elaborated in educational practice, that is, the literacy training method. No one can deny the success of the practice. People learned to read and write in a short period of time. They also became critically aware of the social reality in which they were immersed and took steps to change and control this reality. Yet success in practice does not necessarily mean truth and consistency in theory. One can inadequately explain what one has successfully practiced. A person can also succeed because he does not practice what he theorizes. Freire again and again goes back to the reality of what he did in order to explain his theory as completely and as consistently as possible. He also modified his practice as a result of theoretical and practical considerations. There is in his work, therefore, the close dialectical relationship between theory and practice that lies at the very heart of his educational philosophy.

Freire's theory of learning is subordinated to political and social purposes. Such a theory is open to the charge of indoctrination and manipulation. The situation in which Freire worked in Brazil made him sensitive to these charges, at least to the degree of avoiding conflict with rightist elements in Brazilian society. He is even more sensitive to these charges now that his writings are being examined and considered for application to other countries and cultures. Is the Freire theory of learning necessarily indoctrinative and manipulative? A close look at his writings reveals a certain ambivalence in this regard.

Freire strongly opposes the banking concept of education. He criticizes the primers used in literacy education because they impose ideas on the learners. He insists that the words and the themes to be used in education be those common among the people who are being educated. The content of education is to be determined jointly with the people who are to pursue the learning. Freire specifies that the codifications should be neither too explicit nor too enigmatic. If the codification of existing reality through pictorial form is too explicit, it will take on the character of propaganda and thus prevent critical awareness from developing on the part of the learners. If it is too subtle or enigmatic, it will lose its capacity to provoke thoughtful discussion. Freire answers charges of indoctrination by contending that his goal is to get people to learn by having them challenge the concrete reality of their lives as presented in the codifications. Another view of social reality is not imposed on them, but through discussing a problematic situation they are led to see the true condition under which they live. Through discussion, they also begin to see that the present social reality is not determined but can be changed.

Although Freire is sensitive to the charge of subtle manipulation, it cannot clearly be stated that he totally escapes this charge. For him, there is no neutral education.

> All educational practice implies a theoretical stance on the educator's part. This stance implies—sometimes more, sometimes less implicitly—an interpretation of man and the world. It could not be otherwise. (Freire, 1970b, p. 6.)

This nonneutrality is shown in the fact that out of all the words and themes that could have been chosen for discussion, those are chosen which have the greatest capacity for challenging the existing social reality. The process of conscientization entails for Freire a radical denunciation of dehumanizing structures, accompanied by the proclamation of a new reality to be created by men. Freire is confident that this will come about through free dialogue in which learners and educators participate as equals. Yet is there not a subtle manipulation built into this method, given the lack of education in the students and the obvious political purposes of the teachers? In such circumstances, it would appear most difficult for teachers to satisfy the demands for objectivity and an appeal to rational argument.

The Organization of Learning for Freire

Both Ivan Illich and Paulo Freire address the question of how learning will be organized. Freire writes about the type of educational arrangements that will bring about the new society and be part of the revolutionary strategy. Illich is more concerned with presenting alternatives to present manipulative and addictive educational institutions. Illich's views in this area are far more striking and provocative. Freire's views can easily be assimilated to traditional educational practices.

Freire's educational organization is similar to the method of participant observation used by anthropologists and sociologists. The various steps in this procedure can be briefly described. A team of experts studies a context to arrive at the significant themes and issues in the life of the people of an area. These themes are codified through pictorial representations. People from the area are involved in the choice of these themes, words, and codifications. These circles may have as their purpose literacy education or postliteracy education. The latter has begun to be termed political literacy by Freire. A fuller exposition of Freire's method is found in Freire (1973a) and Elias (1973).

Freire terms this type of educational arrangement "problem posing" education. He admits its similarities to the type of education that was proposed by Dewey and the progressives in the United States. In fact, he readily admits his dependence on democratic and liberal educators. While Freire's procedures are comparable to American progressive educators, the same cannot be said for the theories through which he explains these procedures. Freire uses the terms and concepts of existential phenomenology to explain what takes place in human consciousness and group interaction.

Freire contends that his method of education is non-manipulative. He insists that there is some middle ground between totally free discovery on the part of the individual and the direct impartation of knowledge to individuals, which he views as domesticating and manipulative. He believes that dialogue is this middle ground. His defense is similar to the rationality principle that analytic philosophers have used to separate teaching from manipulation and indoctrination (Martin, 1970, pp. 95–103; Scheffler, 1960, p. 57). His defense, however, is not completely convincing, because of the strong political orientation of his method toward producing definite outcomes in those who participate in the educational dialogue.

Another difficulty with Freire's organization of learning is his exclusive dependence on this one method. Freire seems to imply that any other form of education is necessarily manipulative and indoctrinative. In railing against the authoritarian education that he observed in Brazilian society, he perhaps goes to the extreme of seeing no value in the lecture and direct presentation as educational methods. Moreover, he is not explicitly aware of the possibilities of subtle manipulation that exist even in "free" dialogue among students and teachers.

Another deficiency in his educational approach, one for which he can hardly be criticized, is his failure to consider the education of minors. Freire's methods were developed among adults and precisely in the area of adult education his educational theory has attracted most interest. But a more complete theory would have to consider the arrangements that would be made for the education of minors. The method of teaching devised by Sylvia Ashton-Warner (1963) bears some resemblances to Freire's methods of literacy training. There also exist methods of teaching reading that resemble Freire's methodology. But Freire himself has not addressed himself to how his educational thought would be applicable to the education of children and adolescents.

Freire's method of literacy training cannot easily be used in teaching English. The words of Spanish and Portuguese are generative in a sense that is impossible for English words. English words cannot be decomposed into syllables like the words from more phonetically constructed languages. In applying Freire's method to the teaching and writing of English, generativity would have to be defined in another manner. Those words could be termed generative which, by the process of association, call to mind other words.

The Organization of Learning for Illich

It is most difficult to compare Freire's educational arrangements with Illich's. Illich goes far beyond Freire in devising
an educational plan for his new society. His ideas certainly
suggest alternatives to present arrangements. He proposes
the establishment of four classes of learning networks. The
first network provides access to educational *objects*, such as
books, radios, microscopes, televisions. A second network is
a *skill exchange* wherein students who wish to master a skill
could contact a master who would demonstrate it for the
learner. The third network is *peer matching* on the basis of
common interests. This peer matching would be done
through a computer. The fourth and final network is a *system
of independent educators*. These educators would pursue
jointly determined, but difficult, intellectual tasks. Adminis-
trators of all the networks would be needed, together with
counselors to aid the students in using the networks.

Illich's purpose in proposing these networks is to present
alternatives to schools as we presently know them. Illich
contends that these networks will avoid institutionalizing the
value of learning and will at the same time make learning
both free and incidental. It has already been said that Illich
is having second thoughts on these alternatives to schools as
he begins to contemplate the possible consequences of education on the free market. The danger is that more rigid tests
for competencies might be set up by the business and labor
community, thus leading to even greater social stratification
and class rigidity than result from the present school arrangements. Illich has applauded the Supreme Court decision that
specifies that requirements for jobs are not to exceed the
demonstrated skills needed for that job. Though this decision
may be of advantage to dropouts, it may also lead to greater
control over people by business and labor interests who will
decide job competencies on the narrowest of bases. Greater
control would be exercised presumably because in being nar-

rowly trained for jobs, people would be untrained in critical abilities.

A number of critics who are impressed with Illich's criticism of educational institutions nevertheless maintain that there is only a breaking-down element in Illich and little effort to build (Greer, 1973, p. 11). Greer is right in asserting that when it comes to a vision for the future, Illich is by no means cogent. But he is not right in saying that Illich's call is simply a call to destroy the schools. Illich is calling for societies not to return to a pre–school era, but to go beyond schools to alternative forms of educational arrangements. His point is that some of the most valuable education that takes place occurs precisely through the types of arrangements he describes in his networks. These need to be expanded greatly while schools are greatly decreased. The amount of education thought to take place in schools, he feels, is highly exaggerated, and besides schools have many harmful side effects.

Though Illich's description of his networks shows imagination and boldness, there also appears to be a certain simplicity in his expectations for these networks. He makes the education of all men sound rather simple when he describes it in terms of access to things and people. Illich is no doubt right in arguing for a breakdown of the excessive bureaucratization of education. But his concrete proposals are mere skeletons with a minimum of muscle. Illich has not turned his attention to developing these proposals in later writings and talks, though in "After Deschooling, What?" (Illich, 1971a), he appears to have realized some of the possibly harmful side effects that might result from an implementation of these proposals.

7
The Relevance of
Radical Religious Reformers

In the first six chapters of this book I have compared and contrasted the social and educational theories of Paulo Freire and Ivan Illich. A fruitful means of evaluating these men has been to view them in the light of their religious backgrounds and outlooks. Both men speak out of the religious tradition. They are Christian humanists who engage in radical social, political, and educational criticism. In the course of these chapters my purpose has been not only comparison but also criticism. Many weaknesses in the approaches these men take on key issues have been indicated.

Though I have been critical of their work at various points, I maintain that what they have done has great importance for people involved in areas of religion, social action, political action, and education. The contributions of these two men may be judged by the interest shown in their work by persons both in the intellectual community and in the practical world of education and social action. In this final chapter I will indicate where I feel the importance of these men lies. At times I will be able to speak of Freire and Illich together; at other times I will have to speak of them separately. This is clearly necessary, for there are as many differences between these two men as there are points of agreement.

Radical Religious Reform

In calling Freire and Illich radical religious reformers, I want to draw attention first of all to their critical analyses of the religious institutions of which they are members. Freire and Illich make serious criticisms of institutionalized religion. Their criticism can be termed prophetic. They see themselves calling the churches back to the fundamental thrusts of Christian faith. Both men contend that they criticize religion out of love and in fidelity to the Christian gospel.

Illich's criticism of the churches is truly radical. In many ways churches have succumbed to the temptation to become product-oriented. Too often buildings, membership, professionalization, and specialization have become ends in themselves, to the detriment of more important religious concerns. The American church has also become too much identified with national goals. Illich's trenchant censure of the churches for their failure with regard to Vietnam, Watts, and Latin America can aid in promoting a more critical posture in the churches.

Illich's criticisms of the bureaucratization of the churches is equally valid. Large churches have gathered more and more professional staff. The distinction between laity and clergy has become more pronounced in church polity. Though it appears impossible to eliminate this distinction, as Illich might wish, some movement toward lessening the distance between the two can certainly be made. The same can be said for Illich's strictures against the large size of many contemporary churches. We are witnessing in our time many grass-roots efforts to seek smaller communities of faith where everyone is known to one another and where an intimacy of sharing is a continual possibility.

Freire's criticism of the churches is different from Illich's. While Illich sees the role of the churches as not embracing direct political action, Freire severely rejects the position that churches should be concerned only with spiritual matters. In his later writings he urges the churches of Latin America to take a more active part in the political and social struggles in various countries.

Freire and Illich take different views of political theology. Both appeal to the Christian gospel in support of their positions. Illich attempts to solve this problem by making a distinction between power and authority. The churches should exert moral authority but they should not succumb to the temptation to use political power. Freire apparently does not see this as a valid distinction. For him moral authority must be translated into some form of political power in this world. For him, not taking sides in a political struggle is not a neutral position, but an act in favor of the existing state.

My reading of the Christian gospel to which both of these men appeal indicates that Jesus' assault on the legal tradition not only called into question the dominant values of his society but also challenged the various social organizations that were reinforced by that tradition. He attacked the existing distributions of prestige, privilege, and authority. In Marxist terms he was attempting to change the basic class structure of society. The assault of Jesus on the legal tradition and what it supported was made in an effort to give people power over their own lives and to liberate them from needless oppressive burdens.

The contemporary Christian and the churches also have, as they have in each epoch, the serious problem of determining what movements or political actions should be taken in conformity with the teachings of the gospel. It is obviously difficult to determine in advance what movements are of God. Religious people may differ, and do differ, on whether or not they see God involved in woman's liberation, Latin-American liberation movements, civil rights movements, and other contemporary social, political, and economic struggles. There are no easy solutions in this area. Illich's view of noninvolvement by the churches is unrealistic. Religious institutions will and should continue to identify contemporary struggles as crucial expressions of divine activity, if these struggles offer concrete possibilities of overcoming bondage and oppression and of actualizing ways in which true gospel freedom can be realized. Decisions must be made; mistakes will no doubt be made.

While I view the position of Freire's favoring political involvement of the churches in contemporary struggles as the more acceptable view, I must also confess to some uneasiness about his expression of this view. The danger of any political theology is that it may easily slip into an ideology. Such a theology must constantly be examining the concrete situation to which it wishes to respond. It must be sensitive to changing conditions and to the complexity of the forces within a given society. The simplistic Marxist analysis of society that Freire and other political theologians engage in does not adequately take into account the complexity of modern societies.

While Freire and Illich can be viewed as religious reformers in the sense that they are prophetic critics of the churches, they are also religious reformers in the sense that they radically criticize contemporary society from a religious perspective. The reception that their ideas have received beyond their own religious communities proves that religious prophecy is still possible in secular societies. The religious critic is still able to speak to the modern world in terms of important values preserved in religious traditions.

Radical Religious Humanism

Both Freire and Illich are radical Christian humanists. They are *Christian* humanists because at the heart of their thought is a Christian view of man. In this view man is a finite creature of God. The capability of reflection and freedom of choice is part of man's essential makeup. Man is responsible for his actions. Men should live together in true brotherhood of equality. Freire and Illich are *radical* humanists because they call all human institutions into question on the basis of whether or not these institutions allow for the full expression of man's being and activity.

I have found certain weaknesses in the philosophy of man espoused by these two thinkers. Both men postulate a human essence, preceding all human experiences, potentially creative but repressed and oppressed by manipulative and addictive institutions. I believe that both men ignore that portion of their religious tradition which speaks to the intrinsic corruptibility of man. I have taken exception to the excessively utopian and romantic view of man presented by these thinkers. This view fails to account for present manipulative structures and holds out illusory hopes for a future golden age.

Both Freire and Illich raise but do not adequately treat the question of the relationship of the individual to the group. There can certainly be no definitive resolution of these conflicts. But no adequate humanism can be developed without a more serious analysis of this relationship than is offered by these contemporary thinkers. In their philosophy it appears that individuals are radically good while institutions are radically evil. Illich speaks of some good institutions, but fails to provide adequate criteria for examining them.

A truly radical humanism must examine carefully the individual's many relationships to groups and institutions. The individual draws from the group his sense of identity, *esprit de corps*, his will for communication and willingness to sacrifice. The institution draws from the individual its powers of renewal and adaptation to change, its humanity and humility, as well as its consciousness of the limitations and bounds to all group activities. This tension need not be destructive —under good conditions it can be creative. A radical Christian humanism such as that developed by these thinkers must examine more seriously the types of possible relationships that may exist between individuals and institutions. A rigid view of man is an inadequate criterion by which to examine all modern institutions.

The view of man that Freire and Illich present is far too idealistic and utopian. An adequate view must begin with a concrete realization of man as body and man as animal. Psychologists like Skinner make us keenly aware of this dimension of man (Elias, 1975). Man must be dealt with from the physical, biological, and social levels of being. It is my view that beyond these levels there are also levels of the spirit that can be distinguished, such as endurance, transcendence, creativity, and dialogue. Freire and Illich are strong in their emphasis on these works of the spirit. But they do not integrate this level of man with the physical, biological, and social. They call man to a utopian activity without presenting the obstacles to be encountered along the way. Their ideas have value in telling us how far we have to go in order to achieve the full humanization of man. Their ideas can also be used to evaluate present efforts in arriving at this goal.

Radical Religious Social Criticism

At the heart of the social philosophy of Freire and Illich lies their Christian view of man and society. This vision affords these thinkers a general point of departure by which they can criticize many truly oppressive and manipulative elements in present societies. Religious faith has given them a place to stand over and above the societies that have nurtured them. We usually think of religion as a conservative force in society. But it is also true that religious faiths have been the products of radical thinkers who criticize existing institutions from a more transcendent vantage point.

In their social criticism Freire and Illich are very much Catholic thinkers. They attempt to maintain the rights of individuals but also assert the rights of the collectivity. Illich's position is particularly interesting. His vision of society is somewhat anarchistic, somewhat socialist, and somewhat capitalistic. William Irwin Thompson terms his view a socialized system of anarchic capitalism (1974, p. 33). While Illich wants the values of freedom, equality, and fraternity preserved, he wants this done in a world that is concentric, hierarchical, sacred, and nonmechanistic. This is the medieval Catholic world, in which the person expresses his uniqueness and freedom in being a part of a collectivity.

In the ultimate analysis, I feel that Illich's blueprint for modern society is basically a looking backward to the Catholic medieval society. Society was then renewed through monastic movements. Illich has set up a monastery in Cuernavaca and is looking for followers who will live there and elsewhere a neo-Benedictine life. In other ways he resembles a modern-day Christian Tolstoy looking for his long-lost peasants. Illich has criticized modern institutions, but he has made himself into an institution.

Illich the man is not really expressed in his books. One has to see him at Cuernavaca in his secular monastery to understand what his social criticism essentially is. There on the fringes of modern industrial society he has set up a small enclave in which he can criticize everything that is wrong in society in light of important Catholic and medieval values. This type of criticism makes us realize the limits of our modern industrial institutions and what they have done to our more traditional human values. As a Catholic critic, Illich is working on the very foundation of bourgeois, Protestant society—the school. He is attempting to separate the power of the mind and the person from the power of the school.

A visit to CIDOC in the last analysis is frustrating. One learns there much that is wrong about modern industrial society. But one also becomes convinced that there is no going back to the world that Illich prefers. When a person returns to a large metropolitan city, it appears preposterous to imagine how the world might again be transformed by medieval and monastic ideals. The ultimate danger in preaching these ideals today is that if they were realized on any large scale, this would prepare the way for larger collectives in which basic human freedoms would be seriously impaired.

Paulo Freire's social criticism differs from Illich's. He has introduced certain Marxist elements into his basically Christian social philosophy. He sees oppression in terms of a struggle between the ruling classes and the masses. He distinguishes between ideologies and the institutions supported by them. Freire has come to accept political revolution as perhaps the only effective means of achieving the radical changes that are necessary in Latin America.

The problem with Freire's social criticism is its simplistic nature. Freire deals only in vague generalities. Oppression is never clearly defined. Freire concentrates on the oppression of the poor and fails to deal realistically with oppression as it is found at all levels of society. It is a mistake to see only the poor as the oppressed and all others as the oppressors. A reform movement needs a much broader community of the oppressed.

The religious dimension of Freire's social criticism has served him well in dictating certain human values that must be preserved. The tone of Freire's writings (except when he is involved in phenomenological discourses) is religious and prophetic. Freire often comes through as the religious crusader who is convinced of his goals and strategies. In discussions with him this air of certainty gives way to a more critical examination of the situation. This may be a problem with many people. But in the case of influential thinkers like Freire, this critical analysis is needed.

Radical Religious Political Philosophy

Both Freire and Illich are advocates of revolutions. Yet a great difference exists between the types of revolution that each man proposes. Freire advocates political revolution for oppressed peoples. Illich advocates a cultural or institutional revolution in which voting majorities will come to power and will use legal means to reconstruct the convivial society.

Both Freire and Illich appeal to the Christian gospel to justify the revolutions they propose. Freire explicitly argues that participation even in a violent revolutionary struggle can be justified and even called for by the Christian gospel. He judges the proposition that "rebellion is an act against God" to be a myth imposed by the ruling elites on the masses. He presents God as a Person who calls men to fight against oppression and to struggle with his help for true liberation. He depicts Jesus as a radical who challenged the oppressive ruling elites of his time. He chides the churches for their illusory thinking that they can remain neutral in the social and political struggles of our time.

Illich's call to revolution has all the appearances of a call to join a Christian crusade against pollution, consumption, and growth. The heart of the gospel message for Illich is the call to poverty, nonviolence, and renunciation. Illich calls the Sermon on the Mount the most rational policy for our world today. As opposed to Freire's view, Illich sees no direct role for the church as an institution in this religious and nonviolent crusade. The church is a place for personal and communal spiritual activities. Illich sees no justification, religious or otherwise, for political revolution, especially of a violent nature. This type of revolution does not touch the essential problems of society—the manipulative and addictive nature of modern industrial society.

By contrasting these views of Freire and Illich one can clearly see that the religious tradition can lead persons in different political directions. Though I have been critical of weaknesses in both positions, I do feel that both men stand for important religious and moral values. Illich gives a religious response to many evils of modern industrial society. Some changes must be made if man is to survive. Limitations must be placed on the growth of modern institutions. Heilbroner (1974) has reached conclusions similar to Illich's and has even called for a return to a more collectivist spirit to avoid impending tragedies and catastrophes. Freire's stand on political revolutions as religiously justified and motivated is a needed corrective to a view of religion that casts it into the role of preserving the *status quo.*

Though I am not always happy with the direction of the

political thought of these two Catholic thinkers, I feel that they have shown how political and cultural issues can be intelligently dealt with out of religious traditions and perspectives. Freire has described the political revolutionary as one who is religiously motivated. Illich has presented us with the image of the cultural revolutionary who refuses political power but who still finds ways to influence social and political change. Ralph Nader's refusal to run for political office and his life of voluntary poverty might be an example of what Illich means by the new elites who live a neo-Benedictine way of life. Nader and Illich force us to conceive of a form of politics without the politics of wealth and power. This form may be rooted in a religious tradition and a religious community.

Radical Religious Educational Reform

I have shown that a most fruitful way to examine Illich and Freire is in the light of their religious philosophy and background. This principle of interpretation also holds for their educational criticisms and proposals. At the heart of the educational thought of these men lies a distinctively religious concept of man and society. Both men criticize schooling and education for impairing the freedom that men should be able to express, the equality in relationships that should characterize human society, and a true spirit of fraternity.

I have shown in Chapter 5 how Freire describes three forms of religion, each of which has a corresponding form of education: traditionalist, modernizing, and prophetic or radical. In this way Freire closely associates his educational criticism with his criticism of the churches. Illich sees operating within the schools the same harmful processes he saw operating within the Roman Catholic Church. A professional class has come between students and true learning. The schools determine what true learning is. Education has become a mass-produced commodity.

Now I want to indicate what I feel is the enduring value

of a radical criticism like that which Illich and Freire make of our educational systems. I believe that they are qualified to make these criticisms, based as they are in religious traditions. If one looks at the essential functions of religion and compares these to the functions of education, there is a natural opposition between the two. It is healthy to have this opposition. This accounts for the interest in the educational radicalism of men like Freire and Illich.

Religion tends to wholeness or inclusiveness while education tends toward specialization. Religion is the effort to develop a consistent philosophy of life; it seeks a total view of the world. Although religion does not always maintain a unity or wholeness in the world, it at least tries to hold together the paradoxes, the opposites, and the contradictions of this world. Religious faiths are interested in holding together life and death, heaven and hell, freedom and necessity, good and evil, body and mind.

The thrust in education, on the other hand, is toward specialization. Education tries to put everything in its place. It is given to dividing things with precision. It multiplies categories, subdivides, compartmentalizes. It divides into schools; it separates different subjects; it divides content from method. Academic persons are known by their specialties or subspecialties.

The religious impulse in men like Freire and Illich rebels at the sight of the contemporary school with its excessive bureaucratization, professionalization, and specialization. All of these things break up the unity of the world in which men live. Both of these men oppose these characteristics even when they find them present in church institutions. The radical religious impulse is directed against such compartmentalization of the cosmos, for it appears to them to reintroduce the chaos out of which a true order was fashioned.

Religion tends to emphasize the individual in his small-group relationships while education tends to view men in masses. The nature of man, his destiny, and his relationship with God and others are the fundamental concerns of religions. Religion is a highly personal matter. Personal and spiritual progress is the fundamental aim of religious activity. If man subordinates himself to a group, it is only for the purpose of better attaining his individual goals.

Education has developed a primary aim of promoting the social, political, and economic order. To do this it attends more to men in large numbers. Though many within circles of education advocate the needs and interests of individuals, decisions are ultimately made on the needs of society. Education is funded by society with the hope that the schools will produce good citizens and good workers.

Religious reformers like Freire and Illich react strongly to this massified view of education. They are obviously not alone in their views. Over thirty years ago Jacques Maritain, another religious philosopher of education, severely criticized progressive education for failing to attend sufficiently to the individual. Maritain developed his philosophy from a Christian view of man. In his view the ultimate aim of education concerned the human person in his religious and personal life, not in his relationship to the social environment (Maritain, 1943, p. 15).

Religion deals with symbol, rite, and myth, while education is concerned chiefly with ideas. Symbol, rite, and myth are the constituent elements by which religion transmits its wisdom, witnesses to knowledge beyond the ordinary, and celebrates mysteries that it cannot explain. Direct analysis does not usually provide entrance into the mysteries that religion proclaims. In religion, life is not a problem to be solved by rational means but rather a mystery to be lived in the depths of an individual or a community. Religion is concerned with believing as an act of the entire person or community.

The vocabulary of education consists of ideas extracted from various areas of life. Educational philosophy has become in many circles the careful and systematic analysis of concepts that are used in educational programs and proposals. The competency-based, teacher-education movement has introduced into education the clear and precise language of systems analysis. The history of education is most often a history of ideas that have succeeded in or failed to influence educational thought and practice.

When radical thinkers like Freire and Illich turn to education they bring with them the various modes and expressions of religious life and discourse. Religion tends to be extremely thick and imprecise, with much obscurity, for it deals with the whole of reality and it transcends the nice limits of subjective and objective. Illich's discussion of problems with schooling and society has been found by many to be imprecise, nonobjective, and nondiscrete. The language of Freire, and even more that of Illich, is replete with symbols from the Judeo-Christian tradition in our culture. It is the recurrent use of these symbols that renders the thinking of radical religious reformers difficult and obscure. Yet through these symbols radical religious reformers proclaim that the world and its institutions must not be acknowledged at the expense of the person, nor must the person exceed his proper place in the world.

Religion is concerned with salvation and education deals with learning. All religions emphasize that man can fulfill his destiny or achieve salvation only through a radical reorientation to the world. Religion begins with the need for a conversion or "metanoia." To achieve salvation a man must separate himself from illusions, from blind conformity to nature and to society, and enter into new relationships at a new level of freedom. Salvation comes through moral responsibility, paradoxical believing, and help from beyond man's normal powers. In this view salvation does not consist in learning from teachers or from books.

Education appears to work on the presumption that with a certain body of knowledge a person can satisfactorily achieve his personal destiny and improve society. Henry Perkinson (1968) has spoken of education in the United States as the "imperfect panacea" for all our social ills. The salvation of the human community—racial harmony, economic prosperity, equality of opportunity, political freedom, removal of social ills—is presented as achievable through education and the schools.

This is not the faith of radical religious reformers like Freire and Illich. They proclaim education insufficient for any of these goals. They look to a more radical reorientation of man and society which can only be thought of in terms of religious conversion. They preach the need for a new consciousness which sees possibilities for change in personal energies as these are enlisted through symbols of a deeply religious nature. In the writings of these men the Biblical concept of the Kingdom becomes again a predominant symbol for envisioning man's task in this world.

Religion is ultimately concerned with mystery, whereas education is concerned with knowledge. Whereas education attempts to reduce mystery, religion attempts to go beyond knowledge to mystery. Religion looks to the ultimate mysteries of life which are beyond our ordinary everyday experience. It is concerned with the hiddenness of God. Religion loses vitality when its metaphors harden into ideas, its symbols are broken, and its rites are intellectualized. Religion rejects idolatry because it compromises the essential mystery of life and meaning. This idolatry is not only concerned with objects but also with intellectual ideas or empty symbols or formulas.

Education is concerned with knowledge as a way to reduce mystery. It seeks to measure, to test, and to clarify ideas. There is a form of education that respects the deeper mysteries of life. But education as it is conducted in the schools is an elaborate effort to make sense out of the world, to bring rationality to man's concerns, to solve problem through the scientific method.

Religious radicals like Freire and Illich urge man to have fewer expectations and more hope. Hope is an appropriate response to the mystery of life. Rising expectations are what we expect from the knowledge that is engendered by education. These men prefer to place their ultimate faith in results that are not planned and controlled by men. They have faith in the goodness of man and nature, and in the goodness of a Being who transcends both.

I do not believe that an easy reconciliation is possible between the thrust of religion and the thrust of education. These conflicting emphases cannot be sidestepped. I believe the critique that religious men like Freire and Illich make of our society and especially of our schools is valuable. As radical Christian humanists they raise the human question about our educational institutions. The human question is at bottom both moral and religious. They have challenged us to ask whether or not people are getting from education the sane and satisfying experience they require and deserve. They have questioned the use of educational systems to maintain existing social, political, and economic arrangements which prejudice the interests of thousands of people. They have questioned the intentions of educational institutions, intentions that are often unbalanced, prejudiced, and superstitiously reinforced by years of thoughtless habit.

Though I have found many areas in which to criticize these contemporary radical religious reformers, my efforts have been those of a loving critique. I believe that the radical criticism that comes from the religious tradition raises fundamental questions about all our modern institutions. The solutions they offer to our problems may not always be realistic. But we can ill afford to dismiss the important questions these religious reformers pose about man, society, revolution, and education.

References

Althusser, L. *For Marx.* Random House, Inc., 1970.

Alves, R. *A Theology of Human Hope.* Abbey Press, 1969.

American Psychological Association, *Publication Manual.* Rev. ed. Washington, D.C.: American Psychological Association, 1967.

Arendt, H. *The Origins of Totalitarianism.* Meridian Books, Inc., 1958.

————. *On Revolution.* The Viking Press, Inc., 1963.

Arraes, M. *Brazil: The People and the Power.* Middlesex, England: Penguin Books, Ltd., 1969.

Ashton-Warner, S. *Teacher.* Simon & Schuster, Inc., 1963.

Bell, D. *The Coming of Industrial Society.* Basic Books, Inc., 1973.

Bereiter, C. "Moral Alternatives to Education." *Interchange,* Vol. III (1972), pp. 25–41.

Berg, I. *Education and Jobs: The Great Training Robbery.* Frederick A. Praeger, Inc., 1970.

Berger, P. *The Social Construction of Reality.* Doubleday & Company, Inc., 1966.

Bishop, J., and Spring, J. (eds.). *Formative Undercurrents of Compulsory Knowledge.* Cuernavaca, Mexico: CIDOC Quaderno 1011, 1970.

Bloch, E. *Das Prinzip Hoffnung.* Frankfort: Suhrkamp Verlag, 1959.

Boston, B. O. "Paulo Freire: Notes of a Loving Critic." In S. Grabowski (ed.), *Paulo Freire: A Revolutionary Dilemma for the Adult Educator.* Publications in Continuing Education and ERIC Clearinghouse on Adult Education. Syracuse University, 1972.

Bowers, C. A. *Progressive Educator and the Depression: The Radical Years.* Random House, Inc., 1969.

Bowles, S. "Cuban Education and the Revolutionary Ideology." *Harvard Educational Review,* Vol. XLI, No. 4 (1971), pp. 472–500.

―――. "Unequal Education and the Reproduction of the Social Division of Labor." In M. Carnoy (ed.), *Schooling in a Corporate Society,* pp. 36–64. David McKay Company, Inc., 1972.

Boyd, W. (ed. and tr.). *The Emile of Jean Jacques Rousseau.* New York: Teachers College Press, 1962. (a)

―――. *The Minor Writings of J. J. Rousseau.* New York: Teachers College Press, 1962. (b)

Brinton, C. *The Anatomy of Revolution.* Rev. ed. Random House, Inc., 1965.

Broudy, H. *The Real World of the Public Schools.* Harcourt Brace Jovanovich, Inc., 1972.

Catalog of Publications. Cuernavaca, Mexico: CIDOC Publications, 1973.

Celestin, G. "A Christian Looks at Revolution." In M. Marty and D. G. Peerman (eds.), *New Theology, No. 7.* The Macmillan Company, 1969.

CIDOC Catalog, No. 16. Cuernavaca, Mexico: CIDOC Publications, 1972.

CIDOC Catalog, No. 17. Cuernavaca, Mexico: CIDOC Publications, 1973.

Clasby, M. "Education as a Tool for Humanization and the Work of Paulo Freire." *Living Light,* Vol. VIII (1971), pp. 48–59.

Colonnese, L. M. (ed.). *Human Rights and the Liberation of Man in the Americas.* University of Notre Dame Press, 1970.

―――. (ed.). *Conscientization for Liberation.* Washington, D.C.: Division for Latin America, United States Catholic Conference, 1971.

Cox, H. *The Secular City.* The Macmillan Company, 1965.

Debray, R. *Revolution in the Revolution.* Grove Press, Inc., 1967.

de Kadt, E. *Catholic Radicals in Brazil.* London: Oxford University Press, 1970.

Dewey, J. *Democracy and Education.* Free Press, 1917.

DeWitt, J. J. "An Exposition and Analysis of Paulo Freire's Radical Psycho-Social Andragogy of Development." Doctoral dissertation, Boston University School of Education. Ann Arbor, Michigan: University Microfilms (No. 26,694), 1971.

Diuguid, L. H. "Brazil Wages Two-pronged War on Illiteracy." *The Washington Post,* Section D-3, December 20, 1970.

Donohue, J. W. "Paulo Freire—Philosopher of Adult Education." *America,* Vol. CXXVII, No. 7 (1972), pp. 167–170.

Dreeben, R. *On What Is Learned in School.* Addison-Wesley Publishing Company, Inc., 1968.

Dulles, J. W. F. *Unrest in Brazil.* University of Texas Press, 1970.

Egerton, J. "Searching for Freire." *Saturday Review of Education,* Vol. I, No. 3 (1973), pp. 32–35.

Elias, J. L. "Adult Literacy Education in Brazil, 1961–1964: Metodo Paulo Freire." *Canadian and International Education,* Vol. II, No. 1 (1973), pp. 67–84.

———. "Paulo Freire and Social Learning." *Journal of Educational Thought,* Vol. VIII, No. 1 (1974), pp. 5–14.

———. *Psychology and Religious Education.* Bethlehem, Pa.: Catechetical Communications, 1975.

Ellul, J. *The Technological Society.* Alfred A. Knopf, Inc., 1964.

Eychaner, F. (ed.). *Ivan Illich: The Church, Change, and Development.* Chicago, Illinois: Urban Training Center Press, 1970.

First Encounter of Christians for Socialism: The Final Document. Washington, D.C.: LADOC, 3, 8a, 1973.

Frankena, W. K. "A Model for Analyzing a Philosophy of Education." In J. Martin (ed.), *Readings in the Philosophy of Education,* pp. 15–22. Allyn & Bacon, Inc., 1970.

Freire, P. *Educação como prática da liberdade.* Rio de Janeiro: Paz e Terra, 1967.

———. *La educación como práctica de la libertad.* Santiago, Chile: ICIRA, Calle Arturo Claro, 1969.

————. *Pedagogy of the Oppressed.* Herder & Herder, Inc., 1970. (a)

————. *Cultural Action for Freedom. Harvard Educational Review* and Center for the Study of Development and Social Change, 1970. (b)

————. *Cultural Action: A Dialectic Analysis.* Cuernavaca, Mexico: CIDOC Quaderno 1004, 1970. (c)

————. "Notes on Humanization and Its Educational Implications." Mimeographed manuscript of a seminar: Educ-International—Tomorrow Began Yesterday, tr. by Louise Bigos. Rome: November 1970. (d)

————. "The Political 'Literacy' Process—An Introduction." Mimeographed manuscript prepared for publication in *Lutherische Monatshefte.* Hanover, Germany: October 1970. (e)

————. "Education for Awareness: A Talk with Paulo Freire." *Risk,* Vol. VI, No. 4 (1970), pp. 7–19. (f)

————. "Education as Cultural Action." In L. Colonnese (ed.), *Conscientization for Liberation,* pp. 109–122. Washington, D.C.: United States Catholic Conference, 1971.

————. "The Educational Role of the Churches in Latin America." Washington, D.C.: LADOC, 3, 14, 1972. (a)

————. "A Letter to a Theology Student." *Catholic Mind,* Vol. LXX, No. 1265 (1972), pp. 6–8. (b)

————. "Conscientizing as a Way of Liberating." Washington, D.C.: LADOC, 2, 29a, 1972. (c)

————. "The Third World and Theology." Washington, D.C.: LADOC, 2, 29c, 1972. (d)

————. *Education for Critical Consciousness.* The Seabury Press, Inc., 1973. (a)

————. "Education, Liberation, and the Church." *Risk,* Vol. IX, No. 1 (1973), pp. 34–38. (b)

Freyre, G. *The Masters and the Slaves.* Alfred A. Knopf, Inc., 1964.

Friedenberg, E. Review of *Pedagogy of the Oppressed.* In *Comparative Education Review,* Vol. XV, No. 3 (1971), pp. 378–380.

Fromm, E. *Escape from Freedom.* Henry Holt & Company, Inc., 1941.

―――. *Marx's Concept of Man.* Frederick Ungar Publishing Company, 1961.

―――. *The Revolution of Hope.* Harper & Row, Publishers, Inc., 1968.

―――. Introduction to I. Illich, *Celebration of Awareness.* Harper & Row, Publishers, Inc., 1969.

Gintis, H. "Toward a Political Economy of Education: A Radical Criticism of *Deschooling Society." Harvard Educational Review,* Vol. XLII, No. 1 (1972), pp. 70–96.

Goodman, P. *New Reformation: Notes of a Neolithic Conservative.* Random House, Inc., 1969.

Goulet, D. "Development or Liberation." In T. E. Quigley (ed.), *Freedom and Unfreedom in the Americas,* pp. 1–15. New York: IDOC, 1971.

Grabowski, S. (ed.). *Paulo Freire: A Revolutionary Dilemma for the Adult Educator.* Publications in Continuing Education and ERIC Clearinghouse on Adult Education. Syracuse University, 1972.

Gray, F. *Divine Disobedience: Profiles in Catholic Radicalism.* Random House, Inc., 1969.

Greene, M. "And It Still Is News." *Social Policy,* Vol. II, No. 6 (1972), pp. 49–51.

Greer, C. *The Great School Legend: A Revisionist Interpretation of American Public Education.* Basic Books, Inc., 1972.

―――. (ed.). *The Solution as Part of the Problem.* Harper & Row, Publishers, Inc., 1973.

Griffith, W. S. "Paulo Freire: Utopian Perspectives on Literacy Education for Revolution." In S. Grabowski (ed.), *Paulo Freire: A Revolutionary Dilemma for the Adult Educator.* Publications in Continuing Education and ERIC Clearinghouse on Adult Education. Syracuse University, 1972.

Gross, R. "After Deschooling, Free Learning," *Social Policy,* Vol. II, No. 5 (1972), pp. 33, 37–39.

Gutiérrez, G. "A Latin American Perception of a Theology of Revolution." In L. Colonnese (ed.), *Conscientization for Liberation,* pp. 57–80. Washington, D.C.: United States Catholic Conference, 1971.

Hampden-Turner, C. *Radical Man: The Process of Psycho-*

166   *References*

Social Development. Doubleday & Company, Inc., 1971.

Havighurst, R. J. "Prophets and Scientists in Education." In
D. U. Levine and R. J. Havighurst (eds.), *Farewell to
Schools???* Charles A. Jones Publishing Co., 1971.

Heilbroner, R. L. *Between Capitalism and Socialism.* Random House, Inc., 1970.

————. *An Inquiry Into the Human Prospect.* W. W. Norton
& Company, Inc., 1974.

Horowitz, I. L. *Three Worlds of Development: The Theory
and Practice of International Stratification.* Oxford University Press, 1966.

Houtart, F., and Rousseau, A. *The Church and Revolution.*
Maryknoll, New York: Orbis Books, 1971.

Illich, I. "Puerto Ricans in New York" *Commonweal,* Vol.
LXIV (1956), pp. 294–297.

————. *Celebration of Awareness.* Harper & Row, Publishers, Inc., 1969.

————. *Deschooling Society.* Harper & Row Publishers, Inc.,
1970.

————. "After Deschooling, What?" *Social Policy,* Vol. II,
No. 3 (1971), pp. 5–13. (a)

————. *Ensayos sobre la transcendencia.* Cuernavaca, Mexico: CIDOC Sondeos 77, 1971. (b)

————. "Toward a Society Without Schools." *Center Report,*
Vol. IV, No. 1 (1971), pp. 5–7. (c)

————. *Institutional Inversion.* Cuernavaca, Mexico:
CIDOC Quaderno 1017, 1972. (a)

————. "Deschooling Society." *Colloquy,* Vol. V, No. 2
(1972), pp. 44–48. (b)

————. "How Can We Hand On Christianity?" *The Critic,*
Vol. XXX, No. 3 (1972), pp. 15–21. (c)

————. *Bibliografia Limites,* agosto-septiembre de 1972.
Cuernavaca, Mexico: CIDOC Document, 1972. (d)

————. *Retooling Society.* Cuernavaca, Mexico: CIDOC
Quaderno 80, 1973. (a)

————. *Tools for Conviviality.* Harper & Row, Publishers,
Inc., 1973. (b)

————. *Energy and Equity.* Harper & Row, Publishers, Inc.,
1974.

————. *Medical Nemesis: The Expropriation of Health.* London: Calder & Boyars, Ltd., 1975.

Johnson, C. *Revolutionary Change.* Little, Brown & Company, 1966.

Julião, F. *Cambao—The Yoke, the Hidden Face of Brazil.* Middlesex, England: Penguin Books, Ltd., 1972.

Katz, M. *The Irony of Early School Reform.* Beacon Press, Inc., 1968.

————. *Class Bureaucracy and Schools.* Frederick A. Praeger, Inc., Publishers, 1971.

Kolakowski, L. *Towards a Marxist Humanism.* Grove Press, Inc., 1968.

Komisar, B. P. "More on the Concept of Learning." In B. P. Komisar and C. J. B. Macmillan (eds.), *Psychological Concepts in Education.* Rand McNally & Company, 1967.

Komisar, B. P., and Coombs, J. R. "Too Much Equality." *Studies in Philosophy and Education,* Vol. III, No. 2 (1965), pp. 263–271.

Kozol, J. "Free Schools Fail Because They Don't Teach." *Psychology Today,* Vol. V, No. 11 (1972), pp. 30–36, 114. (a)

————. *Free Schools.* Houghton Mifflin Company, 1972. (b)

Landsberger, H. A. *The Church and Social Change in Latin America.* University of Notre Dame Press, 1970.

Lefebvre, H. *The Sociology of Marx.* Random House, Inc., 1968.

Levine, D. U., and Havighurst, R. J. (eds.). *Farewell to Schools???* Charles A. Jones Publishing Co., 1971.

Ley general de educación. Lima, Peru: Ministerio de Educación. 1972.

Lloyd, A. S. "Freire, Conscientization, and Adult Education." *Adult Education,* Vol. XXIII, No. 1 (1972), pp. 3–20.

Lonergan, B. J. F. *Insight: A Study of Human Understanding.* Philosophical Library, Inc., 1957.

MacEoin, G. "Marx with a Latin Beat." *Cross Currents,* Vol. XXI, No. 3 (1971), pp. 269–275.

Maddox, J. *The Doomsday Syndrome.* McGraw-Hill Book Co., Inc., 1972.

Mannheim, K. *Ideology and Utopia.* Harcourt, Brace & Company, Inc., 1936.

Maritain, J. *Education at the Crossroads.* Yale University Press, 1943.

Martin, J. R. *Explaining, Understanding, and Teaching.* McGraw-Hill Book Co., Inc., 1970.

McClellan, J. E. *Toward an Effective Critique of American Education.* J. B. Lippincott Company, 1968.

Moltmann, J. *Theology of Hope: On the Grounds and the Implications of a Christian Eschatology.* Harper & Row, Publishers, Inc., 1967.

Neuhaus, R. J. *In Defense of People.* The Macmillan Company, 1971.

Occampo, T. *Mexico: "Entredicho" del Vaticano a CIDOC, 1966–1969.* Cuernavaca, Mexico: CIDOC Dossier 37, 1969.

Perkinson, H. J. *The Imperfect Panacea.* Random House, Inc., 1968.

Peters, R. S. *Ethics and Education.* London: Scott, Foresman & Company, 1966.

Petras, J. "Revolution and Guerrilla Movements in Latin America." In J. Petras and M. Zeitlin, *Latin America: Reform or Revolution.* Fawcett Publications, Inc., 1968.

Petrie, H. "Review of I. Illich, *Deschooling Society."* *Educational Theory,* Vol. XXII, No. 4 (1972), pp. 469–478.

Popper, K. *The Open Society and Its Enemies.* Princeton University Press, 1963.

Postman, N. "My Ivan Illich Problem." *Social Policy,* Vol. II, No. 5 (1972), pp. 32, 34–36.

Pratte, R. *The Public School Movement.* David McKay Company, Inc., 1973.

Quigley, T. (ed.). *Freedom and Unfreedom in the Americas.* New York: IDOC, 1971.

Raskin, M. "The Channeling Colony." In M. Carnoy, *Schooling in the Corporate Society,* pp. 23–35. David McKay Company, Inc., 1972.

Rawls, J. *A Theory of Justice.* Harvard University Press, 1971.

Reimer, E. *School Is Dead.* Doubleday & Company, Inc., 1971.

Rosen, S. M. "Taking Illich Seriously." *Social Policy,* Vol. II, No. 6 (1972), pp. 41–46.

Sanders, T. G. "Brazil: A Catholic Left." *America,* Vol. CXVII (1967), pp. 598–601.

Sartre, J.-P. "Existentialism or Marxism." In G. Novack (ed.), *Existentialism Versus Marxism.* Dell Publishing Company, Inc., 1966.

Schaff, A. *A Philosophy of Man.* Dell Publishing Company, Inc., 1963.

Scheffler, I. *The Language of Education.* Charles C Thomas, Publisher, 1960.

Shatz, M. (ed.). *The Essential Works of Anarchism.* Bantam Books, Inc., 1971.

Skidmore, T. *Politics in Brazil 1930–1964: An Experiment in Democracy.* Oxford University Press, 1967.

Skinner, B. F. *Beyond Freedom and Dignity.* Alfred A. Knopf, Inc., 1971.

Sousa Santos, B. de. "Law Against Law." In D. Weisstub (ed.), *Law, Growth, and Technology.* Cuernavaca, Mexico: CIDOC Quaderno 1019, 17/1–17/23, 1972.

Spring, J. *Education and the Rise of the Corporate State.* Beacon Press, Inc., 1972.

———. "Anarchism and Education: A Dissenting Tradition." In C. Karier, P. Violas, and J. Spring, *Roots of Crisis,* pp. 215–231. Rand McNally & Company, 1973.

Stanley, M. "Literacy: The Crisis of Conventional Wisdom." In S. Grabowski, ed., *Paulo Freire: A Revolutionary Dilemma for the Adult Educator,* pp. 36–54. Publications in Continuing Education and ERIC Clearinghouse on Adult Education. Syracuse University, 1972.

Thompson, W. I. *Passages About Earth: An Exploration of the New Planetary Culture.* Harper & Row, Publishers, Inc., 1974.

Tolstoy, Leo. *On Education.* Tr. by L. Wiener. The University of Chicago Press, 1967.

Wagley, C. *An Introduction to Brazil.* Columbia University Press, 1971.

Warford, J. H. "Education, Theology, and Liberation: Reflections on the North American Contest," *Lumen Vitae,* Vol.

XXIX, No. 1 (1974), pp. 91–108.

Weaver, J. F. "Paulo Freire and Education: One Sociological View." Paper Presented at American Educational Studies Association, February 23, 1972.

Weffort, F. "Education and Politics." Introduction to P. Freire, *Educação como prática da liberdade.* Cambridge, Massachusetts: Center for the Study of Development and Social Change, 1969.

Weisstub, D. N. *Law, Growth, and Technology.* Cuernavaca, Mexico: CIDOC Quaderno 1019, 1972.